Library of Congress Cataloging-in-Publication Data

Hebert, Michael R., 1944-
    Insights and strategies for winning volleyball / Michael R.
Hebert.
    p.   cm.
    Includes index.
    ISBN 0-88011-423-1
    1. Volleyball--Coaching.   I. Title.
GV1015.5.C63H43   1991
796.325--dc20

90-25551
CIP

ISBN 0-88011-423-1

Acquisitions Editor: Brian Holding
Developmental Editors: Holly Gilly and June I. Decker, PhD
Managing Editor: Valerie Hall
Assistant Editors: Dawn Levy and Kari Nelson
Copyeditor: Dianna Matlosz
Proofreader: Terry Olive
Production Director: Ernie Noa
Typesetter: Angela K. Snyder
Text Design: Keith Blomberg
Text Layout: Tara Welsch
Cover Photo: University of Illinois Sports Information Office
Cover Design: Jack Davis
Interior Art: Gretchen Walters
Printer: Edwards Brothers

Leisure Press books are available at special discounts for bulk purchase for sales promotions, premiums, fund-raising, or educational use. Special editions or book excerpts can also be created to specification. For details, contact the Special Sales Manager at Leisure Press.

Printed in the United States of America

10 9 8 7 6 5 4 3 2 1

Leisure Press
A Division of Human Kinetics Publishers, Inc.
Box 5076, Champaign, IL 61825-5076
1-800-747-4457

Canada Office:
Human Kinetics Publishers, Inc.
P.O. Box 2503, Windsor, ON N8Y 4S2
1-800-465-7301 (in Canada only)

UK Office:
Human Kinetics Publishers (UK) Ltd.
P.O. Box 18
Rawdon, Leeds LS19 6TG
England
(0532) 504211

Insights and Strategies for Winning Volleyball

Mike Hebert, PhD
University of Illinois

Leisure Press
Champaign, Illinois

Thank you Sherry, Becky, Hillary, and Bunkie.

Contents

Preface

As I browse through the literature on the sport of volleyball, it strikes me that most of the popular works attempt to tell us what to do. They tell players which techniques to use and coaches which drills to run in practice. I find this information extremely valuable, but I also feel a need for something more conceptual—something that surveys the volleyball coaching terrain and provides the concepts by which the reader can pursue his or her *own* conclusions about what to do. This is what I have attempted to contribute with the publishing of this book.

I began this project with the hope that by telling my story, I would be able to provide a step-by-step account of how I drew the conclusions that have shaped my coaching philosophy. I wanted to share my personal reflections and to explain my growth process by revealing the vulnerabilities and mistakes as well as the successes. I wanted the book to be thought provoking. I wanted the reader to be left with concepts instead of recipes. I think I have succeeded.

As I reflect on the manuscript, I am struck by how effectively it satisfies two seemingly remote segments of the coaching profession. On the one hand, it creatively explores several advanced features of coaching volleyball and will be helpful to coaches involved in the highest levels of competition. At the same time, the concepts developed throughout the book can be applied to beginning levels of play.

I begin by providing a brief account of my personal history as it relates to the sport of volleyball. It is a unique history and I believe it will help the reader understand my particular approach to coaching.

The introduction is followed by three technical chapters. In the first chapter, I present my opinions and theories on volleyball offense, culminating with a description of the evolution of the Illinois primary hitter system. In the next two chapters, I explore volleyball defense and make an effort to highlight what I consider its most important points.

In the last three chapters, I chronicle the development of my philosophy of goal setting, program building, and preparing to coach a match. I draw heavily on personal observation and experience as I piece together an explanation of how each of these tasks can be approached.

I feel comfortable recommending this book to the entire volleyball community. Coaches will find it useful because it enables them to confront critical issues in a personalized, nonthreatening fashion. Players will enjoy it because it is well-stocked with genuine encounters with the game and how it can be played. General volleyball enthusiasts will find it an easy, comfortable excursion into their favorite pastime. This book will complement not only the volleyball-specific library, it will also stand as a stimulating exploration into how to approach the art of coaching *period*.

Mike Hebert

How All of This Happened: An Introduction

One of the questions most frequently asked of me over the past few years has been, How did all of this happen? When I arrived at the University of Illinois in August of 1983 I found a program in disarray. We won 5 matches that season, lost 25, and finished dead last in the Big Ten. Four years later we had won our second consecutive conference championship and our first regional championship and had competed in our first Final Four in Indianapolis. We had emerged as, and continue to be, one of the nation's elite programs. I'd like to answer that question—How did all of this happen?—and in the process identify what in my mind are the critical ingredients in building a successful volleyball program.

But first, I think it is important that you understand the unique perspective that has guided my approach to coaching volleyball. The present coaching environment stresses strict training regimens, precise teaching models, correct technique, and exact systems of play. And I wholeheartedly agree that these are imperative if a coach wants to put a competitive team on the floor. But I came upon these concepts only after I had coached for a few years. Early on I faced the coaching task armed with only a seat-of-the-pants orientation that had evolved from my exposure to the sport up to that point.

In 1962, when I transferred to the University of California at Santa Barbara, I was lured to join a fraternity that boasted a "v-ball" court in its side yard. I had been an all-league basketball player in high school—there was no scholastic volleyball of any kind where I had gone to school in San Bernardino, California—and I assumed the fraternity brothers were trying to impress me with the promise of an on-site "b-ball" court. My first clue that I had misperceived the matter came when I heard the guys talking about ordering some more sand to be dumped on the court. I thought I would be shooting hoops on the "b-ball" court, but clearly they were talking "v-ball," which meant sand volleyball, which I had never heard of or seen before.

But I learned quickly. Sand volleyball at UCSB was something of a religion in those days, and we were the early missionaries. We played every day. I can remember on many occasions hurrying to finish a game in time to throw on a T-shirt, brush off the sand, and run to class. On weekends we started at nine or ten o'clock in the morning and played until dark. After the sun went down we would sometimes relocate to a campus indoor facility to get in some more playing time. I estimate now that in a year's time, combining the outdoor play with the indoor doubles and the indoor six-man season, we logged about 1,500 hours of volleyball.

The interesting thing about this experience is how we learned to play the game. Much like youngsters learn basketball by plunging into the highly competitive playground wars, we learned volleyball by playing it. There were few coaches in those days. One learned by modeling the techniques of the better players and by using personalized trial-and-error to develop a set of successful tactics. Like all of the other players, I learned to approach volleyball in a highly instinctive, firsthand fashion. To this day, I make some coaching decisions that seem to fly in the face of reason or are difficult to justify given today's more informed technical and tactical theories. And I make them because I carry with me a very special feel, a deep trust in the instincts that grew within me during those early years of highly competitive "playground" volleyball.

I left UCSB in 1966 to live in Nigeria, West Africa, and to work for the Peace Corps as a science teacher at St. John's Teacher Training College, near Port Harcourt. For the record, I formed and coached the first-ever collegiate volleyball team in Nigeria. I enlisted the students' labor in clearing some land to lay out the court. I worked with a village weaver to come up with an approximation of a net. And the college's physical education teacher called in a favor with a blacksmith friend to design and weld the cast-iron posts we used as standards. The tough part was finding a ball. But through a connection I had developed with the nearby USAID office I was able to lay claim to a brand-new rubber Voit. After a few days of tryouts and team selection, I unveiled the inaugural edition of the St. John's College men's volleyball team.

Finding someone to play against was a real problem. After considerable search, I came upon a group of expatriates who met on Sunday afternoons to play volleyball at one of the European sports clubs. I showed up for a look-see and soon had them talked into forming a team—our first opponent. A big bonus, by the way, was that one of their players, a jukebox salesman from Beirut named Saleem, owned and was willing to share a leather outdoor volleyball. The downside was that they only had five guys and I would have to play with them against my own team. What a scene. There was Antonio, our 5 foot 4 inch setter from Greece; Saleem, our Lebanese outside hitter; Kenneth, a Dutch oil executive; Gunnar, a construction design engineer from Finland who was the other middle blocker opposite me; and some other guy whom I can't remember.

We were lined up against the St. John's team who were equally unique. With only one rubber ball to use in practice one can imagine how unrefined these players' skills were. Suffice it to say that 5 out of 10 attempts to pass or dig a ball, my players would use their soccer skills, either heading the ball or kicking it back over the net. And when they scored a point or a side-out, they would launch into a 60-second celebration, yelling "Goal!" as they danced around the court.

So while others were continuing their careers and expanding their knowledge of the game as it was being played on the beaches and in the gyms of southern California, I was on a fascinating detour through a part of the world that had barely even heard of the sport. UCSB classmates like Dave Shoji, the highly successful coach at the University of Hawaii, were staying closely in touch with the evolution of the game as it was being nurtured in its southern California "cradle." I was trying to scrape off a piece of land, find a ball, weave a net, and locate an opponent—all the while faced with the perplexing task of teaching the game to a group of men who had never seen it played, whose athletic instincts dictated that they kick and head the ball, and who now had to resist the deeply ingrained soccer rules, which forbid touching a ball with the arms and hands.

My purpose in describing these events is not to suggest that my particular experiences prepared me any better or any worse than did the experiences of those who stayed in volleyball's "fast lane." However, I do want you to know that my story is a bit different from most and that my early playing experience coupled with a marvelous intercultural coaching episode caused me to look through some rather unorthodox lenses when years later I was called upon to build the program at the University of Pittsburgh.

But this is getting ahead of myself. I returned to the United States in 1967 to begin my graduate schooling in the philosophy of education at Indiana University. A new arrival, I began searching for a volleyball interest group with whom I could continue my addiction to the sport. At this point, of course, the sunny climes of Santa Barbara and equatorial

Africa had to give way to the artificial lighting of the midwest's indoor gymnasiums. Naturally, my focus narrowed so that I concentrated only on the indoor six-man game. And it was here in the midwest, during the late 60s and early 70s, that I began applying all of those earlier acquired instincts and sensitivities.

I played on a number of United States Volleyball Association (USVBA) teams during those years. And often, usually by default, I had to assume the role of player-coach. This usually meant that I was the guy who collected the money to buy the uniforms and pay the tournament entry fees. But on occasion it meant that I decided who to insert into the starting lineup and made random suggestions as to what system we should use in matches. But this was enough to ignite a spark of curiosity about how these questions should be pursued.

It was at this point in my playing career that I began to look more closely at what others were doing with the six-man game, in terms of technique and tactics. And there was no better area in the country for this to have happened than in the midwest. As I travelled around to tournaments, I met and watched people who were to become some of the greatest volleyball coaches this country has produced. There were Doug Beal and Terry Liskevych at Ohio State. I also got to observe Suguru Furuichi, a Japanese national coach, who spent some time coaching the OSU men's team during those years. A few hours up the road, under head coach Don Shondell, Ball State University's men's team was producing great young coaches like Mick Haley, Jim Stone, and Arnie Ball. In the Chicago area I got to know Jim Coleman and Jerry Angle when they were pioneering the George Williams College volleyball program. It was a fertile time and a fertile region in the growth of American volleyball. It was then and there that I first learned how to look at volleyball from an analytical point of view, to combine intelligence with instinct. I will be forever indebted to my midwestern volleyball roots as I am to my California beach roots. Both have played an important role in shaping my identity as a coach.

In June 1976, I agreed to coach the University of Pittsburgh women's volleyball team. I'd never seen a women's volleyball match. Nevertheless, I accepted the $2,500 part-time salary and welcomed myself to the coaching profession. And as the players returned to campus for preseason training I felt eager and ready for the challenge.

To say that I was ill-prepared to face the events of the next few weeks is to seriously understate the matter. For starters, I held a formal tryout and managed to cut the returning setter from the 1975 team. This kid was 4 feet 11 inches tall and didn't have great hands. I really didn't know the returnees from the newcomers, so I was unaware of just whose name I had placed on the cut list. The next day I learned that she had been the team's starting setter and had received a full scholarship from the previous coach. In the days that followed, I was caught in a storm of complaints from parents, administrators, boosters, and players. In my mind I had made a simple, noncontroversial decision to cut an athlete who, in my judgment, could not help the team. I didn't have a sufficient understanding of the collegiate athletic environment, which includes scholarships, sport governance rules, administrative accountability, community sentiment, and so on. I couldn't believe that a simple roster decision could cause such an uproar. The entire episode was a crash course in learning about the role of the head coach in maintaining good public relations.

A few days later, I met the team for our first practice session. I was nervous, the team was nervous. How were we going to get along? Did the team have any talent? Was the coach going to be a jerk? We never found out, at least not that day. The practice had to be cancelled because the gym had been assigned simultaneously to us and to a basketball summer camp. I had my reservation form in hand, but so did the basketball coach. At that moment, I was introduced to two more axioms of coaching volleyball. The first is that basketball coaches adhere to the belief that their sport occupies a naturally superior position in the universe and will always take priority over volleyball. And the second is that it is essential for a volleyball coach to seek out the person in charge of scheduling facilities and do absolutely anything to get on that person's good side. This is your only protection against these kinds of "scheduling errors."*

When I finally did get to run my first practice session, I encountered my greatest challenge. To put it succinctly, I was in over my head. I must have been quite a sight, with my football-style coaching shorts, my whistle, and my clipboard. After all, my only prior role models had been my own coaches in football and basketball. I tried to talk with a gruff voice. I even threw in a few swear words to make the environment more "athletic." I began practice with basketball's familiar figure-eight drill, the one where three players run a weave from one baseline to the other, shooting a lay-up at the end. Although I made my players catch and chest-pass as they ran through the drill, I am relieved to say that at least I didn't force them to shoot the lay-up!

Then I ran a volleyball-related drill in which I emulated the heartless Japanese coach (from that now infamous piece of videotape) who spiked and threw balls at players until they were reduced to sobbing, battered pulps lying at his feet. One by one I ordered my players to enter the pit for their go at the coach. After 10 minutes or so I had to end the drill. It

---

*You'll find these volleyballs in the margins throughout the book. They indicate that the text delineated by the black line contains an especially important insight.

turned out that I was the only one in the gym getting a sustained work-out, and I was exhausted. Furthermore, I had neglected to organize an efficient shagger-feeder system and had run out of balls. You should have seen the looks my players shot at me as they left the gym.

I'll always remember that group. They were so patient. They probably don't realize it, but they taught me more about coaching than any text-book could have. I learned from them that when teaching motor skills, it isn't enough to tell a frustrated spiker to "Just jump higher and ham-mer the ball!" Nor, in attempting to motivate your team, is it enough to muster a pained expression and implore your team during a time-out to go back out there and *concentrate*, as if that magic word could suddenly propel your players from a 3-12 deficit to go on and win the game. I learned, too, that giving in to the sometimes uncontrollable urge to ex-press feelings of disgust when your players are performing poorly *never* succeeds as a catalyst for improved performance. But most of all, I learned that becoming a successful volleyball coach involves mastering a broad range of administrative, pedagogical, philosophical, and psycho-logical skills—and that in my first days as a coach, I possessed virtually none of these.

In one sense, my lack of formal training in the coaching profession was clearly a detriment. I didn't know a warm-up from a cool-down. And I struggled in the practice gym, without even the most rudimentary understanding of the principles of motor learning and drill management. In another sense, however, my ignorance turned out to be a blessing in disguise. Unfettered by predispositions, I was free to confront with an open mind all of the questions associated with coaching volleyball and to seek my own answers. I've wandered down a few blind alleys over the years, but for the most part, I have grown to like my approach to coaching volleyball.

This is a book written for coaches who want to go beyond the basics, who want to become familiar with the concepts that should guide their decisions in structuring, not only a team's system of play, but the envi-ronment in which that team is to function. But mostly, it is my effort to share some of the important lessons I have learned as I've made my way through over 25 years in volleyball. Much of what I have to say may seem obvious to some, but very little of it was obvious to me. I'm also certain that there are better ways to coach volleyball. But I am content at this point to describe, with some degree of confidence, what I know as my way.

Offensive Tactics and the Evolution of the Primary Hitter System

I can remember the moment I began to appreciate that volleyball offense is situational. Years ago, while coaching at the University of Pittsburgh, I watched my setter run our 3-7-1 play during a match (see Figure 2.1).* The left-side hitter came inside for the 3, the right side hitter looped inside for the 1, and the middle hitter crossed behind the setter for the 7 (see Figure 2.2). We had served and had just passed a free ball to our setter in perfect position. The setter fed the 7 to our middle hitter on the crossing pattern, and she hammered it straight down for a point. Perfecto, I thought to myself.

But when the setter ran the same play later in the game, I had a very different reaction. This time, instead of receiving an easy free ball, we were in the more precarious situation of having to initiate offense from serve-receive. We passed the ball accurately, the setter set the 7, and again the play went down for a kill. But this time it scored a side-out, not a point. Even though the play had been executed successfully, I knew something was wrong, that we had just committed a fundamental tactical error. Despite being comfortably ahead in the score, I called a time-out. I told the team to freeze the previous offensive sequence in their minds and that we would discuss it after the match.

---

*Throughout this book I refer to offensive plays by the numbering we use at Illinois. You can always refer to Figure 2.1 to refresh your memory of our system.

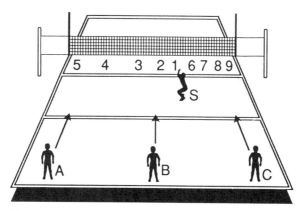

Zones 5, 4, and 9 are fixed permanently on the net:

5 = High outlet set to left side
4 = Looping set to inside left position approximately 6 feet from left antenna
9 = High outlet set to right side

Zones 3, 2, 1, 6, 7, and 8 move in relation to the location of the setter:

3 = Quick set approximately 5 to 6 feet in front of the setter
2 = Approximately 4 feet above net, 4 feet in front of setter
1 = Quick set approximately 1 to 2 feet in front of setter
6 = Quick set approximately 1 to 2 feet behind setter
7 = Approximately 4 feet above net, 4 feet behind setter
8 = Looping set to inside right position approximately 6 feet behind setter

Zones A, B, and C represent back row attack corridors and are permanently fixed in the left, middle, and right positions, respectively.

Figure 2.1 At Illinois, I use the above nomenclature in structuring our offense.

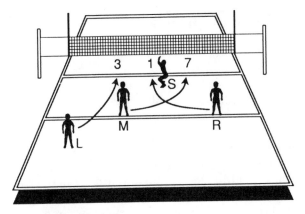

L = Left-side hitter
M = Middle hitter
R = Right-side hitter
S = Setter

Figure 2.2 The 3-7-1 attack pattern.

OFFENSIVE TACTICS

I had allowed my team to approach offense in a homogeneous, one-dimensional fashion. But the reality is that offense is situational in character, requiring different tactical considerations for each situation. In the first instance, we were the serving team, thus each offensive opportunity during that rally was a *point-scoring* situation for us. In the second instance, our opponent had served, and we were in a *side-out* situation. Tactically speaking, this is an important difference.

Side-Out Offense

Once a coach understands the circumstances surrounding the side-out phase of the game, certain conclusions are inescapable. First, side-out offensive tactics should reflect a concern for minimizing errors. Second, all side-out situations begin with the reception of serve and the execution of serve-receive offense. Passing accuracy and first-ball offense efficiency are therefore central ingredients in a strong side-out game. And third, player specialization in both receiving and attacking roles should become a permanent staple in the design of side-out offensive systems.

Low-Risk Side-Out Offense

One consideration stands out from all others in assessing the side-out, or serve-receive offense situation—any mistake will give the opposition a point. Therefore, tactics for serve-receive offense should be designed not only to win the side-out, but also to reduce the potential for error. In other words, serve-receive offense should be low-risk.

Low risk can mean a variety of things. For example, it might involve always setting the hitter with the highest attack percentage. It might mean setting the hitter who is matched up against the opponent's weakest blocker. Or it might mean setting a normally high-risk set that, because of a player's unique talents, make it low-risk for your team. You might have an exceptionally talented quick hitter, for example. Setting a 1 or 3 would be low-risk for your team, but high-risk for most others. You, the coach, must evaluate your players' particular capabilities and determine what is low-risk for your team.

To guarantee the low-risk factor in serve-receive offense a coach should always designate at least one set within each attack sequence as an outlet set. An outlet set is a safe, high set requiring only minimal standards for pass location and setter-hitter timing. Offensive plays without an outlet—plays which consist of only quick or low second-option sets—are high-risk, because they demand a perfect pass as well as perfect timing from everyone in the offensive pattern. To reduce these risks and thereby minimize the chances of an unforced error giving the opponent an easy point, make sure that at least one outlet set is built into each serve-receive opportunity.

This was the tactical error I had sensed from the bench that day. The 3-7-1 sequence had no outlet. Any significant error in pass location or setter-hitter timing would have left us no safe place to set the ball. In that situation, such an error most likely would have cost us a point, either because of an outright mistake in our attempt to force one of the play's difficult options or because sloppy execution would have sent over a free ball. But by replacing the 3 to the left-side hitter with a 5, for example, the play's risk factor is greatly reduced. The new sequence, 5-7-1, maintains the deception and speed of the 7-1 combination, but also allows the setter to select a safer option (5) if necessary.

The low-risk principle is frequently and unnecessarily violated at all levels of play. A central theme in designing a system of play for volleyball should be to find ways to keep an opponent from scoring points. One way to accomplish this is to reduce the potential for error in serve-receive offense by lowering the risk factor.

Of course, it is possible that against certain opponents the low-risk, outlet-oriented offense that I advocate won't work. For example, this conservative approach may not be sufficient to win side-outs consistently enough to beat a good blocking team. In this case, a tactical adjustment from a low- to a higher-risk offense becomes necessary. With the higher-risk patterns comes greater deception, and with greater deception comes an increased potential for beating the block and winning the side-out. At the same time, however, this increased side-out potential is always accompanied by an increase in the risk of losing points through errors in execution. Though high-risk strategies are sometimes justifiable, this does not undermine the legitimacy of emphasizing low-risk tactics when designing a side-out offense.

Serve-Receive Tactics and Side-Out Offense

Another critical factor in determining the success rate of serve-receive offense is passing accuracy. An accurate, in-system pass gives a well-conceived offense an advantage over the defense. The receiving team should be able to win side-outs the majority of the time. On the other hand, a poor, out-of-system pass usually results in an easy-to-read set and allows the defense time to get at least two blockers on the ball and to carefully organize their defensive configuration behind the block. This transfers the advantage to the defense, which should be able to thwart the side-out attempt.

Of course, there are exceptions to this. Some teams are blessed with gifted outside hitters who seem to be able to side-out against almost any defensive alignment. For them, there is no such thing as an out-of-system pass. Lang Ping, star of the world and Olympic champion Chinese women's teams of the early to mid-1980s, was nearly unstoppable on the outside, regardless of the quality of the pass and set. The same has been true for the powerful Cuban Women's National Teams. They push power hitting in women's volleyball to a new level. For them, siding out after a poor pass is not a problem. But for most teams, passing accuracy correlates with success in side-out offense.

Maximize Passing Accuracy

There is clearly some truth to the axiom, Passing determines how well your team is able to play. It seems appropriate, therefore, to address the matter of how to maximize accurate team passing.

Passing Technique. For one thing, it is important that your players possess good technical passing skills. This is an obvious prerequisite, and I am going to leave the presentation of how to teach technical passing skills in the capable hands of my many colleagues who frequently write and give clinics on this topic. I will, however, pass along one observation: Players who demonstrate sound forearm reception skills while playing defense do not necessarily make good passers. And neither does one have to demonstrate classical forearm reception skills to be a good passer.

Defensive receptions normally have one fact in common—the ball, having been attacked in some fashion, is spinning. This means that its trajectory is true and predictable, thereby simplifying the forearm reception task. Receiving serve, however, is more difficult. The popularity of the floater serve is due to the fact that there is no spin on the ball, which means that the trajectory of most serves is unpredictable. The ball can suddenly break as much as 6 feet in any direction, and it can speed up or slow down during its flight. Regardless of the technical purity of their passing form, only players with exceptional eye/hand coordination can become good passers. Look for this attribute first when you evaluate the serve reception potential of your athletes.

Psychological Skills. Psychological skills are also important in maximizing passing accuracy. The dead-ball period leading up to the whistle that initiates the serve produces, in my opinion, more anxiety than any other time during competition. In all other phases of the game, players are moving, reading, and reacting to the multiple, changing cues that characterize the rapid flow of play during rallies. Their minds are occupied with the second-by-second demands of keeping up with the pace of the game. But in this one instance before play begins, with players standing in place, waiting for the triggering effect of the serve, negative and unproductive thoughts can invade the receiving team's side of the net.

Players understand that passing errors are, after all, errors of the worst kind. They lead directly to the opponent's scoring a point—and with only one contact of the ball! The *thought* of committing a passing error can easily evolve into fear, and as each player falls prey to this fear, the situation can escalate into a full-blown team anxiety attack. I know; I have seen it happen at all levels of play. It begins with one player's uncertainty as to who should pass the serve that hits the seam. Then another player begins to wonder whether or not to encroach into another player's zone to receive a ball, as yet another player begins passing scared—freezing up and praying that a teammate will come to the rescue by passing any ball that comes near.

Solutions to this problem are elusive and require that a coach pay close attention to how and when these anxieties occur. I offer one generalized suggestion: Passing should be instinctive. Coaches should avoid focusing on the pressure of the serve-receive situation. If I close my eyes, I can easily call up the image of the coach who, after seeing the team blow a pass, stands up to plead with the players, ''Come on, *concentrate* out there . . . *Think* about what you're doing.'' This only accelerates the anxiety-producing process. Instead, coaches should encourage players to get their minds off the anxiety of serve-receive. Though I can offer no scientific evidence, it seems that teams whose coaches provide positive leadership and display a quiet confidence in their players' ability to recover from errors are able to avoid the prolonged passing breakdowns prevalent among teams whose coaches' pained expressions and anxiety-provoking comments only draw attention to errors.

Serve-Receive Formations

How a team positions its players to receive serve can also influence passing accuracy. Coaches must decide how to cover 81 square meters of court with a maximum of five receivers (one player normally is assigned setting responsibilities and is not part of the receiving formation). There are several variables to consider in designing serve-receive formations. First, a coach must evaluate the capabilities of each player as a potential receiver. How much territory can the player cover and how accurately can he or she pass? And what areas of the court should be covered or left open? The height of the men's net is 8 feet, and the women's net is at 7 feet 4-1/4 inches. The trajectory of the serve over the women's net will tend to be lower and straighter. Does this mean that receiving formations for women should be different from those for men? Should a coach design one formation and strive to execute it to perfection, or would it be better to gain flexibility by teaching more than one formation?

The W Formation. The history of team receiving tactics presents a clear, evolutionary picture. It has been dominated by one particular formation, the W formation (see Figure 2.3). Its rationale seems to be that all available players are needed in the receiving formation in order to cover as much of the court as possible. Each player is assigned to a particular area

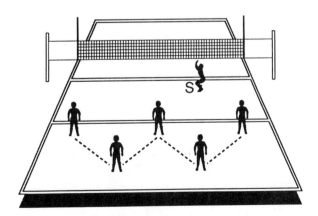

Figure 2.3 The W formation.

of the court. Normally, the two back row passers receive the majority of serves. Front row receivers guard against the short serve. Seam responsibilities—receiving a serve directed at the area between two receivers—are predetermined by assigning one of the two players on either side of the seam to pass the ball. This has proved to be a very clean, tidy system, which still exerts a major hold over team receiving tactics worldwide and at every level of play.

Variation on the W Formation. During the first few years of my coaching career, I accepted the W formation, as did most coaches, as the only practical way to receive serve. In fact, I became critical of those who did not adhere to this conventional wisdom. I can remember watching the Peabody High School (Pittsburgh) boys' teams in the mid 1970s. They were the perennial city champs (high school volleyball was and still is very popular and played at a high level in the western Pennsylvania area) and were coached by a good friend of mine, Joe Silipo. Joe would line up his team to receive serve and use three and sometimes just two receivers. Not only that, he used the same two or three kids to pass every ball. There were always two or three nonreceivers whose task was to stay out of the way of the primary passers. This was heresy, of course, and I remember the sense of responsibility tugging at me, urging me as Joe's friend to diplomatically clue him in to the fact that the W formation—with an occasional change to a four-man pattern—was indeed the proper way to align a team to receive serve.

As it turns out, Joe was light-years ahead of me. For whatever reason—and I am certain that Joe had a very specific one—he had determined that his team passed better with this highly unorthodox system. Six years later, our USA men's national team pioneered this same serve-receive specialization concept as they prepared for their gold medal effort at the 1984 Olympic Games. Joe understood then what it took me years to understand— a coach should never feel bound by convention or tradition in designing a system of play. I watch volleyball matches at all levels of play, and I see some seemingly crazy things going on out there on the court. At one time, I would have seen these things as signs of how little these coaches knew. Now I look more closely to discover why a certain tactic is being used. I have developed a deep faith in coaches' abilities to be creative.

As with other phases of the game that I had accepted as part of volleyball's ingrained conventional wisdom, the more I coached the W formation, the more I began to have doubts about its capability of maximizing passing accuracy. After a period of hard work ironing out problems in the structure of the W system, I realized that the real problem may be the system itself. It occurred to me that no matter how proficient my team became using the W formation, I still had no say in which of my players would be in the high percentage, back row receiving positions. Instead, this was determined by the chance positioning of players as they rotated through the receiving positions of the W. This was a serious drawback, and I began to look for alternate strategies for receiving serve.

Specialization in Serve Reception

I felt very strongly that which players line up in the high percentage receiving positions should not be left to chance but should be based on the passing skills of each player. Outfielders aren't called upon to become relief pitchers in the bottom of the ninth, and defensive tackles aren't asked to play wide receiver. Why should I ask all of my players, some of whom did not possess good passing skills, to become passers? I began to define this postulate: The number of receptions by good passers should be maximized, and the number of receptions by weak passers should be minimized. I felt that a good passer could be more effective covering a larger area than could a weak receiver covering a smaller area. I realized that instead of relying on one standard receiving formation, such as the W, I had to design a *variety* of formations, and that each formation had to place the team's best passers in the high percentage receiving positions. Weak passers could be placed in the low percentage, front row positions or be moved out of the receiving formation altogether.

Identifying the Best Passers

The first step was to identify the team's best passers by recording each player's passing statistics in practice and competition. I then studied each rotation to determine how receiving formations could be designed to maximize the number of receptions by my best passers. In one rotation, for example, we would line up in a three-receiver formation (see Figure 2.4a). The players in Positions 4, 5, and 6 were all good passers. The players in Positions 2 and 3 were weak passers and were stationed at the net. Figure 2.4b shows the same team three rotations later. The weak passers are now in Position 5 and 6 and again are out of the receiving formation, this time near the baseline. This still leaves three good passers available for receiving responsibilities. It didn't matter to me that my receiving formations were not alike in each rotation, nor that I sometimes had my nonpassers at the net and sometimes near the baseline. I felt like I was beginning to gain tactical control over the serve-receive phase of the game.

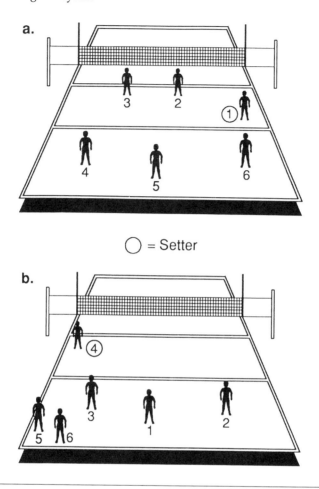

Figure 2.4 The three-receiver formation (a). The three-receiver formation after 3 rotations (b).

Changing Formations

It also occurred to me that a coach should have a specific move, a tangible adjustment available to help a team recover from team passing breakdowns. I felt that one such move could be to change formations after a passing error. Multiple receiving formations would have to be designed for each rotation, and knowledge of these formations would be so exact that, on a given signal, the entire team would shift immediately into the corresponding alternate. There are three potential advantages to this tactic. First, the player committing the error is able to set up in a different receiving position and isn't a sitting duck for the next serve. Second, as players move to a new position, they are forced to engage mentally in something other than worrying and can meet the next serve with a renewed mental outlook. And third, the opponent's server is presented with a new "look." This reduces the probability that the server can simply hit the same serve for another easy point.

The decision to change formations was based on a sound knowledge of my team's passing efficiency in each rotation. By compiling thorough statistics, I discovered in which rotations my team passed well and in which they passed poorly. I tended to change formations after each passing error in the poor passing rotations and to wait longer in rotations that had been more successful. Coupled with my earlier decision to design formations that featured the better passers, the strategy of changing formations further bolstered my confidence as I sought to implement tactics for improving my team's passing accuracy.

The Passing Specialist

I brought both concepts with me in 1983 when I began coaching at Illinois. First, I wanted my best passers to receive every serve. And second, I wanted my team to have adjustments available to them that would aid in preventing team passing breakdowns.

It was at this point that I got lucky. Simultaneously with my individual search for reliable serve-receive tactics, the USA men's national team—again under the innovative influence of Doug Beal and his collaborator, Bill Neville—was introducing to the world a revolutionary strategy for the reception of serve. These new concepts gave fuller expression to the embryonic instincts that had been guiding my own thought processes. I was a mere reformer who was trying to improve the W concept. Beal and Neville were genuine revolutionaries calling for the scrapping of the W altogether.

Specialization, they argued, is a concept that must be applied to volleyball. Traditionally, we had asked players to be well rounded and to excel at every skill. This is not only impossible, they said, but it isn't even desirable, at least when it comes to designing serve-receive formations. They junked the five-person W formation for two reasons. First, it assumes that everyone is equal in passing ability, and this is not likely. Second, and this was an insight that had not fully registered with me, the W formation presented far too many areas of confusion. If you glance again at Figure 2.3, you will notice the seams, both vertically and horizontally, that exist between receivers. A substantial number of passing errors, they believed, occur when a server attacks one of these seams. There is always an uncertainty, even when seam assignments are made very clear, that has to be overcome before a successful pass can be executed.

As a result, Beal and Neville decided to create a new position—the passing specialist. In their scheme, only two players would be assigned to pass the ball, and it would be the *same* two players in every rotation. This ensured that only their best passers were receiving the serve, and the number of confusing seams was reduced to only one. The remaining players were given other responsibilities, such as calling "in" or "out" to aid the passing specialists in their attempts to receive serves headed for the sidelines or the baseline. The USA system utilized their two outside hitters as passing specialists, and they received virtually every serve as the USA team won two consecutive Olympic gold medals (1984 and 1988). Moreover, they were considered to be one of the best passing teams in the world. Specialization in the serve-receive game had made a major impact on the sport of volleyball.

Advantages of Specialization

The advantages of this system are significant. First of all, only your best passers are contacting the ball. Because they receive in the same two-person formation in all six rotations, these two players become accustomed to playing together. They begin to sense each others instincts. The result is increased clarity with regard to which player will take the serve and therefore, a decrease not only in seam aces, but in overall aces by the opponent. Another advantage is that the quick attackers, freed from receiving responsibilities, can channel all of their attention toward their hitting assignment. This leads to improved offensive execution. Settling on a lineup, too, becomes an easier task. The decision to start the great net player with poor passing skills, a real dilemma for coaches employing the W system, presents no problem at all for the team using serve-receive specialists. And finally, the amount of time devoted to serve-receive practice, a major chunk of time for most teams, is dramatically reduced for teams employing specialization. This time can now be used to refine other parts of the game.

Applying the Specialization Principle

Before running off to design two-person receiving formations for your team, you should consider the following caution. Specialization requires that you have on your roster at least two players who have sufficient passing ability to execute the system. Furthermore, your team passing statistics should be higher using the passing specialists than in any other serve-receive formation. Otherwise you would be missing the point. Beal and Neville utilized the specialist system because their team passed better this way than any other way. In fact, and I'm quite sure Beal and Neville would agree, your responsibility as a coach is to create a passing system that enables your team to pass as accurately and consistently as possible, whatever that system may be. They have provided a revolutionary concept, serve-receive specialization using two outside hitters to pass every ball, and would urge you to modify it to fit your own circumstances, with regard to talent and level of play.

Let me illustrate: In 1984 at the University of Illinois, I was anxious to apply the specialization concept to my receiving patterns. Through a series of statistical evaluations, I determined that I had two players who were talented passers with great instincts. The problem was that one was hitting outside and the other was a middle blocker. This meant that they would not be opposite each other in the rotational pattern and that, unlike the USA national team, my receiving formations would have to be asymmetrical. It also meant that my quick hitter would have to back off the net to pass in her three front row rotations, not something I was particularly excited about. But the fact is that my 1984 Illinois team compiled the best passing statistics any of my teams have ever recorded, before or since. And the reason was that I happened to have two players who were great passers in the open court. I borrowed the concept of specialization and moulded it to fit my own situation.

Two years later, I was forced to make yet another modification. I didn't have any "pure" passers on the team. They were all decent passers, but no one player stood apart from the others as had been the case in 1984. So again I modified the specialization strategy to fit the situation. I decided to keep the idea of receiving with two players, but they were not going to be the same two players in each rotation. Because my players were roughly equal in passing ability, it was no longer important to design formations that featured the same two passers. Instead I designed formations that maximized our setter penetration and attack efficiency, and then I assigned passing responsibilities to two of the remaining players in each formation. Even though we were no longer using passing specialists in a pure sense, we did maintain the fewer seams/less confusion advantage of the two-player receiving formation.

By the beginning of the 1987 season, I was comfortable with the notion of modifying concepts to fit the situation. This was good because my 1987 team at Illinois, a team that went all the way to the Final Four, was clearly not a good passing team. It wasn't because we didn't work on passing technique. Nor was it because we didn't have good athletes on the roster. We simply couldn't pass the ball well as a team. I started that year trying to pass with two outside hitters. Out of frustration I moved another player into the formation so that we passed with three players—two players in the normal deep receiving areas and one player covering the short zone on the left or the right side of the court, depending on the particular rotation we were in at the time. When this didn't improve our passing statistics, I tried using four receivers in an arched configuration. We finally began to pass better as a team.

Upon investigation I learned that our improvement was due not to any superior feature of the four-player receiving pattern, but to the fact that the players felt more confident having more areas of the court covered by a potential receiver. For this particular team, then, the psychology of the formation was more important than its tactical strategy. So here I was—a coach that three years earlier had become committed to the principle of passing specialization and had used a two-player formation successfully, returning to a multiple-player receiving system. The important point here is that tactical concepts, no matter how exciting and revolutionary they may seem in the abstract, can be applied successfully only if your athletes can execute them. I am still a believer in serve-receive specialization, but I also stand ready to design alternative serve-receive tactics if I am forced by circumstances to do so.

Before moving on, I would like to address a criticism that has been aimed at those, like myself, who advocate specialization in the serve reception phase of the game. I have proposed on many occasions that specialization be implemented at all levels of play, including scholastic and junior development levels. Good passers, in my opinion, should be identified at an early age and encouraged to become passing specialists. Scholastic and junior coaches often counter that this would be unfair to young players who are nonpassers. Many of these coaches feel that they have an obligation to produce well-rounded players and that any decision to specialize should wait until after this developmental period is over. Though I understand this sentiment, I feel strongly that the passing specialist is here to stay, just as the setter position, for example, is here to stay. We have come to accept the fact that setting is a specialization that is essential to the modern game. We no longer train every player to become a setter. On the contrary, we identify setters at an early age and ask them to play that position exclusively. The passing specialist position will evolve to the same status. It is only a matter of time.

Offensive Compatibility and Serve-Receive Formations

One concept remains in evaluating tactics for maximizing the efficiency of side-out offense: A side-out offensive system should be compatible with the positioning of attack players mandated by the receiving formation in use. In fact, an offensive system should not only be compatible, it should maximize the offensive potential created by those attack positions.

For example, in the conventional W receiving formation, the position of the front row attack players is inflexible. In the back row setter rotations, the three attack players are evenly spread across the court just behind the attack line. These players must hold their receiving positions after the serve and not release into their attack routes until after they are certain that they do not have passing responsibilities. By holding their receiving positions, these attackers reduce their approach options to those that have their respective receiving positions as starting points. Figure 2.5 depicts the traditional, straight-ahead tendencies, with occasional crossing patterns (e.g., A2), which characterize serve-receive offense run from the W formation. The front row setter rotations allow for more diversity in that the two front row hitters can line up to receive serve in a stack-left, stack-right, or split configuration, but the commitment to hold to an assigned receiving position limits the hitters' attack options in the same fashion.

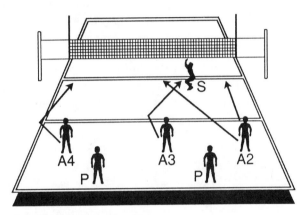

A = Front row attackers
P = Back row passers
S = Setter

Figure 2.5 Serve-receive offense run from the W formation.

Furthermore, the rotation rule means that in two out of three rotations, any team using the W is forced to give up whatever attack specialization roles it has cultivated. Most teams deploy two left-side hitters, two middle, and two right-side players (at least one of whom is a setter). This means, for example, that the person passing and hitting from the left-front position is going to be a left-side hitter in one rotation, a middle hitter in the next rotation, and a right-side player in the next. In two out of every three side-out offensive opportunities, players will be asked to attack outside their areas of offensive specialization. Quick hitters will be asked to hit high sets, and outside hitters will be asked to hit quick sets.

Many teams employing the W formation have devised tactical adjustments to get their hitters attacking the sets best suited for their respective talents. One common example finds the middle hitter (receiving in the left-front position) coming inside for a 1 set, and the outside hitter (receiving in the middle-front position) looping outside for a 5 set. Nevertheless, the restrictive effect of assigned receiving positions, combined with the disruptive nature of the rotation rule, have placed some very real limitations on the design of side-out offensive tactics for teams using the W formation.

Now consider the offensive possibilities for teams using some form of serve-receive specialization. One common feature of these systems is that the front row middle hitter is not asked to pass. This means that the middle hitter, freed from the distraction of receiving serve, can stay near the net and focus immediately on attack responsibilities. I have found that this leads to markedly better execution by middle attackers. It also means that this attacker, not held to any serve-receive position, can roam freely to initiate an approach and hit any set from any area of the net.

Attack options for outside hitters are also seen in a new perspective when using serve-receive specialization. Compared to players receiving in the narrowly structured W system, front row passers soon become less territorial as they maneuver around the court to pass and get into an attack pattern. A front row passer, lined up to receive on the left side of the court, may move all the way to the right side to pass a particular serve. This could spell trouble if a play has been called requiring the passer to move straight ahead to hit a 5. But a more flexible offensive concept that allows this player to approach the 5 set using an inside-out move, or to audible to a set on the right side of the net would be more compatible with specialized passing formations.

The point is that for every receiving formation, there is an offensive system that amplifies the offensive capabilities inherent in each formation. Combined with the concepts of minimizing risk and maximizing passing accuracy, the notion of compatibility should be addressed in designing tactics for side-out offense.

Point-Scoring Offense

Point-scoring offensive opportunities suggest a different frame of mind, described vividly in this excerpt from the USA Men's National Team Player Manual distributed to team members in the early 1980s:

> The key to our point making transition philosophy is, when the opportunity to score points is presented through a dug ball, down ball, or free ball, the team—every time—works to get into hitting positions so that we can mount our maximum attack. Point making transition is an attitude. The attitude is that if we create or the opponent gives us the opportunity to score, we will, with maximum impact.

Transition Offense Can Be Higher Risk

Commonly referred to as transition offense, these point-scoring opportunities differ from side-out situations in that errors result in losing only a side-out, not a point. (The recent rule change resulting in rally scoring in the deciding game will invalidate this analysis for Game 5 of a match.) Furthermore, successful execution of the offensive play will, in fact, *earn* a point. Because losing a side-out is not as severe a penalty as losing a point, and because a team should maximize any possible opportunity to score a point, higher-risk offensive plays are more tolerable, perhaps even more desirable, during transition situations. This is why I applauded our use of the 3-7-1 pattern during the transition opportunity in the earlier example.

Another reason to advocate the higher-risk, quicker-developing attack patterns in transition is that these offensive opportunities always begin with attack reception. Whether the opponent has just pounded a high velocity spike into your defense or has floated a free ball into your easily organized receiving pattern, your team now has the chance to mount a counterattack before the opponent can convert from offense to defense. In other words, the defending team has the chance to gain the advantage, and the goal of every team should be to develop its counterattack before the opponent can organize a defense.

One way of accomplishing this, at least when the attack reception is controllable, is to lower the trajectory and increase the velocity of the pass so that the setter receives the ball as quickly as possible. Then move immediately into one of the quicker-developing combination patterns, setting up one of the quick options. By minimizing the elapsed time between the first pass and the final attack, the offensive team increases its chances of gaining the advantage over a slower reacting defense.

Transition Offense Must Be Flexible

Another important consideration regarding transition offense is that, depending on their defensive position prior to the upcoming attack opportunity, the location of attackers at the outset of each sequence may vary. As a result, hitters may find themselves in awkward positions for attacking certain sets. A middle hitter may, in one instance, call for a 3 set in transition. This involves a relatively easy movement pattern if M has just blocked against an attack from the opponent's Area 2. However, a much more difficult movement pattern for hitting a 3 is required if M has just blocked against an attack from Area 4. In another example, L may be an outlet hitter normally assigned to hit a 5 in transition. The movement pattern is simple if L is coming from a crosscourt defensive position against an attack from Area 4. A very difficult transition approach pattern is required if L has gone to the floor in the center of the court in an emergency move to bring up a tip.

One way to cope with this problem is to allow the out-of-position hitter to audible to an attack pattern that more accurately fits the situation. The quick hitter who is late getting into the offensive flow as a result of having blocked against a wide set on the right side can audible to a 6, in order to ensure a more manageable attack route. And the outlet hitter, after playing the tip in the middle of the court, can audible to hit a 9. This would still be an outlet set and would provide an easier movement pattern. Because of the unpredictability of defensive positioning, it is inevitable that variations in attacker deployment will occur. It would be wise to build a degree of flexibility into transition offensive tactics to allow for last second adjustments in attack routes.

Transition Offense Doesn't Apply Only to Scoring Situations

I should point out that the term *transition offense* can be confusing. It is commonly applied only to point-scoring situations. However, many transition opportunities occur during rallies that have been initiated by the opponent's serve. These are not point-scoring situations. Yet, because they occur during the transition from defense to offense, they tend to be treated in the same fashion as point-scoring opportunities. All of the tactical considerations described here can apply to this category of transition offense, except one. A mistake is not merely a side-out; it means loss of a point. The risk level must be monitored carefully. The setter must always be aware of whether the situation is a side-out or point-scoring one. In side-out transition situations, I recommend a compromise between low- and high-risk offensive patterns. Emphasize the higher-risk, quicker-developing options when your team's ball control and execution is sufficiently precise to get a step ahead of the defense. And stay with the lower-risk sets when circumstances and ball circulation are less controlled.

Coverage Offense

Two additional offensive situations warrant brief discussion. The first can be called coverage offense. This situation occurs when an attack attempt is blocked back into the attacking team's court, and the attacking team is able to cover the ball and prepare for another attack.

At the outset, one usually finds that both teams are bunched near the point of attack. The attacking team is deployed in its offensive coverage formation, and the defensive team has sent two blockers to the ball.

Because only one contact, the block, is used to return the ball into the attacking court, the transition time available to each team is very short. Within this brief time span, however, the blocking team must rebalance its defense, and the coverage team must deploy for its next attack. Two attack strategies suggest themselves. First, assign one hitter—any hitter—to approach for a quick set. The chances of beating the block are excellent. Or second, set *away* from the original point of attack. Few teams are capable of rebalancing their block and backcourt defense quickly enough to be in good position to defend against this type of set.

Out-Of-System Offense

The second offensive situation is one that does not necessarily capture the imagination of the offensive theorist but, because it is frequently encountered, requires strategical attention. It is volleyball's broken play, the out-of-system play that results from an errant first pass.

The unpredictability of ball location makes it difficult to design a consistent set of tactics. However, there are certain rules of thumb that apply. First, when the setter is not able to establish position under the pass, there must be a formula for determining who will set. Each player must be alert for this situation and be prepared to set, if necessary. Second, it is important that your players know the highest percentage set to execute from each area of the court. Third, attackers must be ready to adjust their angles of approach. In this situation, sets often come to the hitter from an unusual point. In order to maintain proper hitting position in relation to the ball, the angle formed by the line of the set and the hitter's approach must be kept optimal (see Figure 2.6).

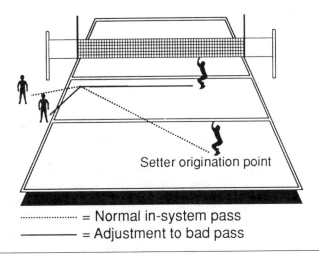

Setter origination point

·············· = Normal in-system pass
———— = Adjustment to bad pass

Figure 2.6 The line of the set and the hitter's approach must be kept optimal.

Fourth, because the hitters must track a set coming from an awkward angle and therefore cannot see the opponent's block as well as they could under normal circumstances, shot selection becomes very important. Discourage hitters from banging blindly into the block. Instead, encourage them to hit high and deep into the vulnerable areas of the defense. This will reduce the chances of the blockers "cherry picking" for an easy stuff.

Despite its unpredictable nature, out-of-system offense should not be left to random chance. These guidelines will help to restore order to what might otherwise be an unstructured offensive situation.

Summarizing Side-Out and Point-Scoring Offense

Understanding the situational character of volleyball can lead to a series of tactical design considerations.

- First, teams must play in a low-risk mode when in side-out situations.
- Second, a team's system of serve reception plays a major role in determining the success rate of its side-out offense.
- Third, a team's side-out offensive tactics should be compatible with its serve-receive formations.
- Fourth, a team should cultivate a point-hungry atmosphere in situations where errors result only in a side-out.
- And finally, speed and efficiency should be built into transition situations, because the advantage swings decisively to the offense if an attack can be executed before the opponent can fully organize its defense.

Tactical Objectives and Set Selection

I can recall my first attempt to bring order to the issue of set distribution in my offensive system. I was coaching at Pitt in the mid-1970s, and I was becoming increasingly frustrated with the seemingly random, undisciplined pattern of set selection that characterized our offense. It wasn't the setter's fault. I simply hadn't provided enough direction. So I decided on this strategy: I ranked the attack percentages from top to bottom for each hitter in each rotation. In Rotation 1, for example, my left-side hitter was hitting .284, my middle hitter was at .305, and the right-side player was hitting .214. Based on these statistics, I decided that in Rotation 1, the sets were to be distributed 50% to middle, 40% to left, and 10% to right. A similar formula was worked out for each rotation. I reasoned that the ball should be set most often to the hitters who had demonstrated an ability to score.

It was with a sense of accomplishment that I introduced these new guidelines at the next practice session. I was certain that the team would feel an immediate sense of pride in the fact that their offense would be governed henceforth not by whim, but by a set of rationally determined principles. Instead, they struggled through their worst practice of the season. I learned later that the players who had been relegated suddenly to a marginal role in the offense were shocked and insulted. What I had enthusiastically presented as an improvement in our offensive system had been perceived as a personal attack against the lower percentage hitters, who felt they were being arbitrarily frozen out of the offense.

I was caught off guard by their reaction. But on reflection I realized that the entire episode was a revealing barometer of the low level of offensive sophistication that I had allowed in my program. My attempt to regulate set distribution according to ability had been met head-on by the prevailing attitude that set selection should be governed by the rule of fair and equal distribution, even if this rule did not make sense tactically. Despite the temporary emotional disruption that accompanied this episode, my team eventually accepted these new offensive guidelines and managed to win two Eastern AIAW championships. In the process, I grew to appreciate a fundamental offensive principle that baseball managers have known about for years—it is better to have your .330 hitter swinging at the ball than your .230 hitter.

Basis for Set Selection

The more I thought about offense, the more I realized that set selection could be subjected to analysis from a variety of vantage points. First, as revealed by my previous experience, a setter can distribute sets based on the demonstrated success rate of each hitter in each rotation. A second basis for determining set selection can be found in the scouting report on the opponent. For example, your setter might choose to set the .230 hitter instead of the .330 hitter, if the .230 hitter is matched against a poor blocker. Or perhaps the setter could choose to feed the .230 hitter on the right side, because the opponent is using a blocking system that is vulnerable to an attack from Area 2. In both cases, set selection is determined more by information about the opponent's block than by the attack capabilities of the hitters.

A third basis for set selection can be found in various play combinations. Most blocking schemes are designed to put at least two blockers against every attack. Combination plays have in common the goal of regaining the offensive advantage by giving the hitter a one-on-one (one hitter against one blocker) swing. It is the setter's job to select the option that will produce the one-on-one situation.

Spreading the Block

One popular play concept is to spread the block by using attack patterns that tend to increase the distance between two potential points of attack, thereby making it difficult for two or more blockers to combine on a multiple block. The most frequently used of this type of play in three-hitter formations is the 3-8 spread. In Figure 2.7, for example, M approaches for a 3 set and R stays outside to hit an 8. Both sets are low and quick, making it impossible for B3 and B4 to move as a tandem to block them. The pressure is on B3, who must commit to blocking either the 3 or the 8. If B3 commits to the 3, then the 8 is set to R, who should be one-on-one. If B3 elects to forego committing to the 3 in order to be in a position to help B4 against the 8, then the setter fires the 3 to M. The key to the success of this play is the setter's ability to anticipate the movement patterns of B3. The same effect can be achieved in two-hitter formations by replacing the 8 set with a C set to the back row hitter in Position 1.

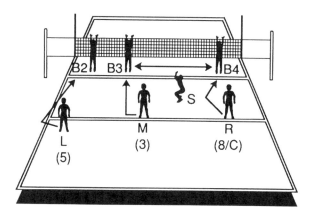

Figure 2.7 The 5-3-8 spread.

Another frequently used tactic is to spread B3 and B2. This can be achieved easily in the two-hitter formations by assigning M to hit a low set behind the setter. If B3 goes with M to block the slide 8, then the setter pushes a low 5 to L, who will certainly be one-on-one against B2. In three-hitter rotations, the same effect can be achieved by running M and R in any combination behind the setter (see Figure 2.8).

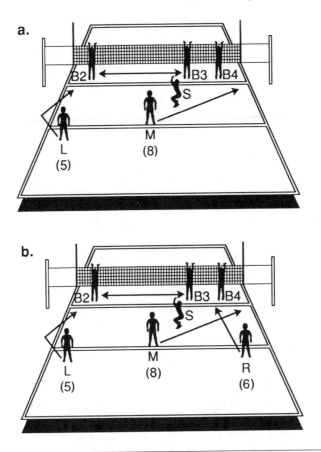

Figure 2.8 Two hitter 5-slide spread (a) and three-hitter 5-8-6 spread (b).

Disrupting the Timing of the Block

A second play tactic is to overload the blocker with a two-set timing combination that will force the blocker to commit to one set or the other, thereby leaving one of the two sets open for a free swing. These plays usually involve a quick set, followed by a second-option set that is slightly higher, but not enough to allow the blocker time to recover from a jump against the quick set and still jump against the second option. Figure 2.9 illustrates one of a variety of X, or crossing, patterns that are widely used by teams at all levels.

If B3 commits to block the 1, then the setter gives the ball to R on a 2 set. The timing of the play is such that R should be able to attack the 2 set as B3 is descending from the attempt to block the 1. On the other

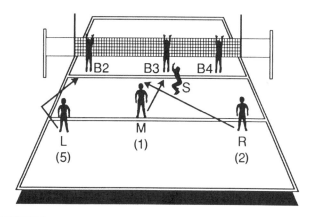

Figure 2.9 Using the right X to overload block.

hand, if B3 does not commit to the 1, then the setter delivers the 1 to M. If the play is executed correctly, B3 cannot stop both the 1 and the 2. This overloading effect can be achieved using any combination of hitters at any zone along the net. Again, the success of the play depends on the setter's ability to set the correct option.

One-Hitter Deception Patterns

A third play concept can be found in the various one-hitter deception patterns that have become popular. These plays are aimed at disrupting the rhythm and timing of the block, thereby giving the advantage to the hitter. Most common among this type of play are the pump fakes used by the quick hitters. M approaches for a quick set, plants, and throws the arms upward as if to jump for the attack. But before jumping, the hitter hesitates, recoils, and jumps a second later to attack a slightly higher set. The intended result is that B3 has ''bought'' the pump fake and is descending just as M is ascending to hit the ball. Pump fakes can be executed in one attack zone, as described, or the hitter can fake in one zone and hop to an adjacent zone to attack. For example, M could pump fake to hit a 3 and hop inside to hit a hanging 1 set.

Selecting which hitter to set requires, first, that the setter become aware of the various rationales justifying set selection. Selection can be based on knowledge of your own hitters' strengths, knowledge of the opponent's vulnerabilities, knowledge of tactical concepts, or on any combination of the three. Your setter must enter each competition with a specific game plan detailing how to decide which hitter to set and how this particular setting pattern can defeat the opponent. Otherwise, your offensive system is left to drift aimlessly, without any control over its tactical effectiveness.

THE EVOLUTION OF THE PRIMARY HITTER SYSTEM

It has been common for coaches to design their offenses around the concept of plays. A list of plays would constitute a team's in-system offense. Typically, these plays are memorized and signaled to each player by means of a prearranged system of communication. A team's playbook might look something like Table 2.1.

Table 2.1 Sample Offensive Playlist

Play	Set		
	L	M	R/BR
1	5	1	9/C
2	5	1	2
3	5	3	8
4	2	3	9/C
5	3	1	9/C
6	2	1	9/C
7	5	7	1
8	4	3	6/C
9	3	4	6/C
9	3	4	6/C
10	7	1	4/A

Note. R is the set assigned to the right-side attacker in a three-hitter rotation. BR is the set assigned to the back row hitter in a two-hitter rotation.

Though this list may be brief, it represents the kinds of offensive patterns run by teams who employ prearranged, memorized plays. When the play is called, everyone carries out a specific assignment. The play must unfold in a strictly consistent fashion so that the setter knows where each hitter will be. Preoccupied with the often demanding task of establishing good position under the pass, it would be difficult for a setter to react to an unannounced, last-second change in a hitter's approach pattern.

Attack Options and the Rise of the Audible

This rigid interpretation of offense began to soften in the 1970s as the concept of options *within* a play evolved. The right-side attacker in Play

2 (Table 2.1), for example, could have the option of hitting a 2 or a 7 off the quick hitter's 1, depending on the location of the opponent's middle and left-side blockers. If the block is cheating inside to stop the 2, the hitter, deployed in a neutral position behind the setter, breaks right to hit a 7. If the block is leaning outside to stop the 7, the hitter breaks left to hit a 2. This particular play was perfected by the Polish men's Olympic team as they pioneered the option concept all the way to a gold medal in Montreal (1976).

One necessary component in the execution of the option play is the audible call by the hitter. The hitter's read on the block occurs too late for the option call to be made before executing the play. Only by the hitter's calling out two or seven as the ball is being passed can the setter know which option to set.

The use of audibles has enjoyed even more widespread popularity than the option concept. Seeking a solution to the problem of offensive diversity in the transition game, coaches saw in the audible call a chance to execute a different attack pattern during each offensive thrust in the long rallies. This was a difficult proposition using hand signals and relying on the memorization skills of each player. But the audible was easily adapted to the transition game and now is used in one form or another by most teams.

I liked the creativity and deceptiveness of the option concept. I liked the quick tempo and diversification afforded by the audible system. And I liked yet another by-product of this particular stage in the development of volleyball offense. In orthodox play-memorization systems, the decision of which hitter runs which pattern was made, in effect, by the setter. Once the setter called the play, the hitter was locked into the approach pattern assigned for that particular play. But as options developed and more and more teams utilized the audible system, an increasing degree of responsibility for choosing hitter approach patterns was falling on the shoulders of the *hitters*. The setter still had the ultimate responsibility of choosing which hitter to set. But the hitters, by being able to make reads and initiate audible calls, began to play a more decisive role in determining the overall configuration of the offense. I liked the fact that the task of deciding how to use the offense, how to select the correct offensive tactics to beat a particular opponent, was becoming a shared responsibility and not left for one person, the setter, to bear.

Evolution of the Primary Hitter System

This was a time during which my own views of volleyball offense were in a percolation stage. Most offenses seemed unimaginative to me. The play-memorization format discouraged flair and creativity. The attack sequences outlined in the playbook became repetitive and stale and more defensible as the match wore on. This was particularly evident during rallies with multiple in-system attack opportunities when it became clear that, as a result of cumbersome play-calling systems, teams were forced to repeat the same offensive pattern over and over.

It also seemed to me that offenses were awkward in taking advantage of opponent weaknesses. Say, for example, an opponent started its left-front blocker in an inside position to help block against an anticipated quick attack. One obvious tactical response would be to freeze that blocker by faking a quick 1, then set a 7 or an 8 to a hitter on a crossing pattern. This would probably catch the left-side blocker leaning inside, giving the crossing hitter a good chance to score on the right side. But to get this matchup, the setter would have to scan the playbook, pick the play that could best exploit this vulnerability, call the play, and then set the correct option. All this takes too much time and relies too heavily on the setter's ability to pluck the right play out of the hat at the right time.

In general, I didn't like the fact that offense was almost exclusively setter-determined. Of course, coaches usually confer at length with their setters before and during matches. But on the floor, during the flow of play, the setter controlled every aspect of the offense. I couldn't understand why this entire burden was placed on one person. Why shouldn't this responsibility be shared? With each swing, the hitters were storing feedback about which sets might or might not work. But under setter-controlled systems, there was no formal way for the hitter to provide this valuable input.

My enthusiasm for investigating different approaches to offensive theory was at an all-time high. I scrutinized virtually every offensive concept I could get my hands on. Slowly, over time, I began to identify those concepts that I felt were valid. By 1983, when I took over the University of Illinois program, I was able to begin constructing the conceptual basis for the offensive system that has been utilized by my Illinois teams ever since.

Three Contributing Principles

To me, three things seemed to stand out. First, an offense should be designed so that a team can get the ball as often as possible to its highest percentage hitter, who then hits the ball into the zone that is least likely to be defended adequately by the opponent. Second, hitters should share in the decision regarding which attack pattern to run in a particular situation. And third, an offense should be creative, flexible, and responsive to rapidly changing circumstances as they evolve during each rally.

Strength Versus Weakness Principle

As obvious as the first concept may seem, it is one which has been little understood even by some "high-level" coaches over the years. In football, the quarterback throws to the primary receiver or hands off to the team's top running back most of the time. Other players share in the offense, but, in the end, the stats normally show that the top players carried the load. In basketball, offenses are designed to get the ball to the top scorers. And in baseball, the team's highest-average hitters are positioned in the top and middle portions of the lineup, in order to get as many "at bats" as possible. However, this concept of maximizing the effectiveness of the top offensive players has not been as prominent in volleyball.

One reason, of course, is that an in-system pass is required if the setter is to have a choice regarding which hitter to set. Most out-of-system passes by necessity are set to the team's outside hitter, even though the outside hitter may not be the team's highest percentage hitter. But I would wager that a random survey of even in-system offensive opportunities would reveal a somewhat less-than-unanimous support for the strength-against-weakness principle.

Let me give a brief example to illustrate my point. Years ago I was watching a men's collegiate volleyball match. Team A began the match with their middle blockers employing a read system, meaning that they were waiting to *see* the ball set to the quick hitter before they would jump to block. One of the advantages of the read-block system is that the middle blocker cannot be faked into the air by a quick hitter and therefore is able to read the opponent's set and move to block at the point of attack, wherever it might be. The disadvantage is that if the set goes to the quick hitter, the blocker may not be able to react in time to stop the quick set. In other words, the quick hitter has the advantage when the blockers are in a read mode.

Team B received the first serve and ran a complicated double-quick, double-crossing pattern where the middle hitter goes for a quick 1, the left-side hitter crosses behind the setter for a 7, and the right-side hitter crosses in front of the setter for a quick 3. They set the 7, two blockers were up, and, intimidated, the hitter waffled the ball out-of-bounds. Team B received the second serve, ran the same play, and set the same hitter. This time, he got stuffed for another point. To my amazement, Team B ran that same offensive sequence three more times and with the same result—points for Team A. At 5-0, Team A finally committed a serving error to end the run.

Afterward, I got my chance to talk to Team B's coach, whom I had known for years. Why, I was interested in knowing, did your setter call the same play over and over? And after seeing that Team A was in a read-block system, why did he play right into the blockers' hands by setting the higher option, the 7, instead of setting the 3 or the 1? Because, he told me, his team really liked running that play. They had worked all week on it, had been particularly effective with it in practice scrimmages, and were determined to get it right in the match. Apparently, it didn't matter that the play, and in particular the option they were setting, was ill-suited for the defensive alignment his team was up against. The opponent's read-block system, the loss of five consecutive points, the predictability of his team's side-out offense—none of these things seemed to be as important to my friend's tactical outlook that night as "getting it right."

Certainly I am not saying that every coach I observed in those days was guilty of such nearsightedness. But this kind of thinking was more widespread than most observers realize. I've had occasion to chat with setters, male and female, over the years and have been shocked many times to hear their justification for calling a certain play or setting a certain hitter. "I didn't set her [the team's leading hitter] tonight because she pissed me off in practice last week." Or "I run that play a lot because I like it." Or "I always try to distribute the sets evenly to each hitter . . . that way no one can say I play favorites."

In recent years, I am happy to report, I have seen a dramatic improvement in the use of sound, offensive tactics. But in the mid- to late 1970s, when I was searching for offensive direction, the concept of matching offensive strength against defensive weakness was nowhere near the top of volleyball's list of items to consider when formulating an offensive game plan.

Shared Responsibility for Set Selection

My second observation, that hitters should share the play-calling responsibilities with the setter, derives from my view that hitters are just as capable of synthesizing information and making calls as setters are. It's not that hitters have been completely frozen out of this activity. Most setters learned to converse frequently with hitters during time-outs and dead-ball periods asking advice on, for example, what play might work in a particular rotation. But I felt that the hitters' status as contributors to offensive tactics should be upgraded and that their role should be formalized and built into the offensive system.

Adaptable Offense

The third concept, that offense, particularly transition offense, should be more adaptive to changing situations, was not hard to conjure up.

While serve-receive offense was becoming the focus for much of the innovative experimentation going on, transition offense remained trapped within the restrictive conceptual confines of the play-memorization format. I had grown accustomed to watching my women's collegiate teams confront, on the average, 135 to 140 offensive opportunities a match. At least half of these occurred in the transition phase. In other words, 65 to 70 offensive opportunities were being executed without much thought being given as to how concepts like diversity, deception, flexibility, and adaptiveness might enhance the scoring punch of the offense. I wasn't prepared to continue living with such a major flaw in my offensive philosophy.

The Primary Hitter System

The 1984 season was approaching, and I began to feel that it was time to get out the drawing board and design an offensive system that would satisfy the conceptual concerns that I had been nurturing during my first 8 years of coaching. I had a freshman setter, Disa Johnson, coming in to run a very young team (8 freshmen, 1 sophomore, and 2 juniors). There would be ample time for this group to internalize my offensive concepts and to provide evidence as to whether or not they were valid. With this in mind, I set myself to the task and came up with an offense that I called the primary hitter system.

The Primary Hitter

In each rotation, one hitter is designated as the primary hitter. The primary hitter should be the highest percentage hitter in that rotation, the hitter to whom you would most like to set the ball. In this system, the primary hitter triggers the offense by making the first call. Looking over the opponent's block and defense, the primary hitter decides which set would provide the best chance to score. The setter picks up the call and, assuming the pass is in-system, sets the primary hitter in the desired location.

The Secondary Hitter and the Concept of Complementary Sets

The secondary hitter in each rotation makes a call *after* the primary hitter's call. The secondary hitter's call must be complementary to the first call—''complementary'' in the sense that, together, both are consistent with the principles of good offensive tactics. One tactical principle, for example, dictates that the offense should be able to keep the opponent from getting two or more blockers to the point of attack. This can be accomplished either by spreading the attack options so far apart that the opponent's middle blocker must commit to one or the other, or by directing a timing combination at one zone to force the block to commit to either the quick or the second option. In both cases, the middle blocker must guess which hitter is going to be set, and assuming the setter selects the correct option, the hitter should be swinging against only one blocker. A 4 set and a 5 set, therefore, would not be complementary, because they are both high sets to adjacent zones. The defense would have no trouble getting at least two blockers up against either set. But if the primary hitter were to call a quick set, a 1, and the secondary hitter were to call something higher, such as a 2 or a 7, then the complementary principle would be satisfied. The same would be true if the primary hitter were to call a high set, a 5, and the secondary hitter were to call something quick, such as a 1 or a 6. The possibilities for complementary combinations are numerous, of course. But the point is that in this system, the secondary hitter has the responsibility to make the next call complementary to the initial call of the primary hitter.

The Outlet Hitter

The last attack role in the primary hitter system is that of the outlet hitter. In each attack sequence, there must be an outlet, a high safety set, available to the setter in case of an out-of-system pass or a breakdown in the development of the quicker options. The outlet hitter, normally the left-side hitter, receives a large number of sets during a match. It is not necessary for the outlet hitter to call a set. The outlet hitter is deployed in an outside attack position, ready to approach and swing at a high set whenever it comes his or her way.

In serve-receive situations, the hitters make their calls using hand signals. During the dead-ball period before the serve, the setter glances first at the primary hitter to pick up the call. The secondary hitter, also reading the primary hitter's call, decides on a complementary set and flashes the second signal to the setter. In transition situations, the plays are called using audibles. In any in-system transition situation, whether playing an easy free ball or digging a hard spike, the primary hitter calls the set as the ball is being passed. The secondary hitter processes the first call and quickly audibles a complementary call. This may seem difficult at first, but I assure you that after only a brief period of practice, the setter and hitters begin working together smoothly.

I turned my 1984 Illinois team loose with this offense, and the results were quite remarkable. After a year of learning to execute it, we improved dramatically in every offensive category. Through the 1985, 1986, 1987, 1988, and 1989 seasons, during which we won 163 matches and lost only 25, the team's overall attack efficiency was .295. We ranked fifth nationally in 1986 with a .300 percentage, second in 1987 with a .302 mark, eighth in 1988 at .287, and second again in 1989 with an even .300 efficiency. Mary Eggers, our all-American quick hitter (who, incidentally, was one of the primary hitters in our offensive scheme) led the nation in attack efficiency in '86 (.455), '87 (.443), and '88 (.433). The primary hitter system was piling up some impressive numbers.

Assigning Roles in the System

I apply the primary hitter system to my 5-1 offense in the following fashion. In the three-hitter rotations, the middle hitter is assigned to the primary hitter role, the right-side player is the secondary hitter, and the left-side hitter will attack the outlet set. In the two-hitter rotations, the middle hitter is the primary hitter, and the outside hitter is the secondary hitter. The outlet duties are shared by the outside hitter, who releases from swing patterns when there is an out-of-system pass, and the back row hitters.

I also stand ready to reassign roles during a match. For example, if someone other than the player originally assigned to be primary hitter starts to get on a roll, I immediately make that player the primary hitter and ask the setter to feed her the ball. The original primary hitter becomes the secondary hitter, and the system remains intact. The hitters have switched roles, but the concepts are the same.

Advantages of the System

The advantages are obvious, at least to me. First, the team's highest percentage hitters receive the majority of the in-system sets. And they get to attack these sets in the zone of their choice. This promotes a high level of confidence in both the hitter and the team. Second, the burden of play calling is taken away from the setter. There are no memorization requirements. The hitters take on an active role in set determination, thereby freeing the setter to concentrate on the important task of selecting which hitter to set. Third, the system is extremely flexible and adaptable. It provides an easy mechanism for hitters to locate and attack the opponent's vulnerabilities. And fourth, the use of audibles allows a team to present a different offensive "look" with each thrust during lengthy rallies with multiple offensive opportunities. The system appears complicated and unpredictable to opponents and scouts, but remains simple and very *un*complicated to those who execute it.

There are two additional advantages. First, the system is not difficult to teach or to execute. The fact that some of its principles are unorthodox causes some coaches to raise an eyebrow. How can a team run a smooth offense, they ask, with hitters yelling out different numbers just as the setter is about to set the ball? Pang WuQiang, former coach of the national champion Shanghai Women's Team and the Dutch Women's National Team, spent the 1986 season on my staff at Illinois. "This is not possible," he said, after listening to a description of the primary hitter system. But after watching his first practice session, he nodded in agreement that the system not only had some merit, it was easily executed. The final proof for me, however, lies in the fact that my players unanimously prefer the feel, the involvement of this style of offense over the passive, mechanical nature of more conventional systems.

And second, the concept of "plays" is modified under the primary hitter system. There are no memorized set plays. Instead, plays are replaced by the concepts of *primary*, *complementary*, and *outlet*. It is these concepts that motivate and shape a team's offensive personality, not a list of restrictive, memorized plays. And though most coaches might feel more secure using the conventional play-calling systems, I encourage them to consider giving their players more offensive freedom. The primary hitter system is applicable to any level of play. I think you will find that, not only will your players adjust to these concepts quickly, they will find it restrictive and boring to go back to more conventional formats.

Wrap-Up

Volleyball offense may have had its conceptual beginning in that moment when the first-ever, instinctive but unplanned spike was launched into the opponent's court. But the intervening years have witnessed the evolution of a highly complex collection of offensive principles. We have seen the appearance of a specialized division of labor between setter, attacker, and passer. We have seen the emergence of intricate language and communication systems. And we have witnessed the development of various tactical concepts, the application of which give a team its offensive personality.

This history, seen in its entirety, serves as the textbook for any coach seeking to design an offensive system. Coaches must first understand that which has already evolved. Then, supplied with a working knowledge of offensive principles, they will be freed to explore their own creative instincts when building offensive systems appropriate to their teams' individual needs and circumstances.

Important Concepts in Developing a Defense

Volleyball defense has evolved into two separate but highly interrelated components—blocking and floor defense. The block is the first line of defense, and its purpose is to block the opponent's attack at the net. Floor defenders are positioned in the defensive court behind the block, and their purpose is to keep the ball from hitting the floor. It is the coordination of block and floor defense that makes up an overall system of defense.

Before the Japanese offensive innovations of the 1960s, volleyball defense had not been forced to contend with a great deal of offensive deception and therefore remained simple in concept. Blocking against the traditional high, outside attack meant that a team had to station one blocker on the right side, one on the left, and one in the middle to move laterally to form a double block, depending on which way the opponent set the ball. Floor defenders were positioned behind the block in areas that gave the defense the best possible chance to dig this high, outside set. The game was slow and deliberate by today's standards and required only minimal strategies for organizing the defensive phase of the game.

But the appearance of the Japanese system of attack changed all that. The intent of this new philosophy of attack was to deceive and neutralize the block and to keep floor defenders off balance by varying the speed and height of the sets. Using three basic principles, the quick attack, the multiple-timed attack, and the multiple-approach attack, the Japanese hoped to spring hitters loose at the net to hit against only one blocker, or perhaps against no block at all. The deliberate, predictable rhythm of the orthodox "high" game was being replaced by the less predictable, staccato-like rhythm of this faster, more deceptive style of play. Traditional defensive schemes were no match for these offensive innovations. It took several years of trial and error before volleyball defense began to catch up with offense. It is safe to say, however, that today's state-of-the-art defenses have addressed virtually every recent offensive innovation. The result has been an explosion in the theory and tactics of defensive volleyball.

BLOCKING

I would like to present the central concepts that have shaped today's defensive theories. But in doing so, I will separate blocking concepts from those that pertain primarily to floor defense.

Positioning the Block

Accepting the principle that it is always desirable, if not always possible, to have at least two blockers at the point of attack, (the first tactical decision in designing a defense must be where and how to position the block in relation to the attack.)

Attack Blocking

In this style of blocking, both blockers move to the point of attack and jump with the intention of reaching aggressively with both hands (into the angle if the hitter goes crosscourt, or out to the antenna if the hitter swings line) to stuff the ball back into the opponent's court. The objective of attack blocking is to move the hands wherever necessary to intercept the attack at the net, thereby preventing the ball from being driven into the defensive court.

At higher levels of play, where the power and velocity of the spike diminish the chances of its being dug by floor defenders, attack blocking has become a popular and often necessary tactic. Coaches at this level feel that their teams have a better chance of blocking the ball than digging in the backcourt. I might also be tempted to use an attack block system at a lower level as well, if, for example, my team were composed primarily of taller players with reasonable blocking skills but only marginal skills as floor defenders. Again, my team's chances of digging the ball in the backcourt would be much lower than our chances of stopping the ball at the net.

The advantage of the attack block is that one contact of the ball can terminate play and result in a point or side-out for the blocking team. The disadvantage is that, in the event the ball is not blocked, floor defenders have a difficult time making accurate digging reads behind blockers who are reaching and moving their hands in a last-second attempt to stuff the ball.

Area, or Channel Blocking

At levels of play where the power and velocity of the spike are more moderate, area, or channel blocking, can become an effective strategy. The objective is to establish the block in a predetermined position in relation to the point of attack, thereby taking away a certain area of the court and forcing (i.e., channelling) the hitter into another area. This style of blocking relies on blocker discipline and on the defensive abilities of the floor defenders playing behind the block.

The advantage of this tactic is that the floor defenders know in advance which area the block will defend and can position themselves with relative certainty in the unprotected areas of the court. Coaches who feel their team's backcourt defensive skills are good enough to dig an opponent's attack often prefer the consistency and predictability of the area blocking system. This would also be an effective blocking system, for example, for a team composed primarily of shorter players with only marginal blocking skills, but who possess above average defensive skills.

Line-Versus-Crosscourt Spectrum

Implementing the concept of area blocking requires that a decision be made regarding how much line or how much crosscourt angle the block should take away (see Figure 3.1, a and b). To establish the location for a double block, the outside blocker normally sets up first; then the middle blocker moves to an adjacent position to form the block. In blocking the line, the outside blocker's inside hand sets up opposite the center of the ball, and the middle blocker closes to form a double block. In blocking crosscourt, the outside blocker's outside hand should set up opposite the center of the ball. In establishing a neutral, middle-of-the-road position, the outside blocker's hands should be placed equidistant from the center of the ball.

Notice that as the blockers' position in the line-versus-crosscourt spectrum varies, so do the unprotected areas of the defensive court. Deciding

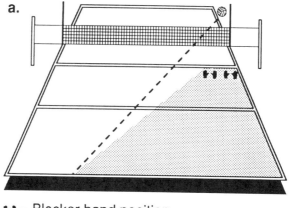

⊷ = Blocker hand position
🏐 = Ball
░ = Area protected by block

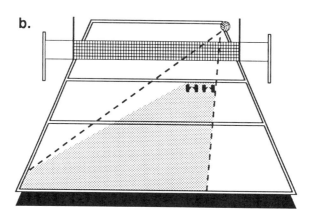

Figure 3.1 Blocking line (a) and crosscourt (b).

exactly where to position the block can be influenced by several factors. On a team whose left-back defensive players possess better ball control skills than its right-back players, blocking line and channelling the opponent's left-side attack into Area 5 would make good tactical sense. Against a hitter who prefers to attack crosscourt, it might make sense to block the crosscourt angle and force the hitter to go down the line. I think there is great tactical merit in frustrating hitters by forcing them to hit less preferred shots.

I offer the following account as an illustration of the tactical effectiveness of positioning the block. My 1985 Illinois team qualified for the

NCAA tournament. For our first round opponent, we drew an exceptionally talented team from Western Michigan University. After hours of viewing videotape, I began to notice how much they relied on their fine all-American outside hitter, Sarah Powers. I also noticed that she preferred to hit the ball crosscourt, even when the block tried to take it away. She was so talented that against this crosscourt block set-up, she merely jumped a little higher and found new and more radical crosscourt angles to attack. After closer evaluation, I saw that even when a line block set-up gave her a wide variety of crosscourt angles to attack, she tended to narrow her focus and hit the same hard shot to the same spot on the court.

I decided to go against "the book," which says that you block crosscourt against a powerful crosscourt angle hitter. I positioned our block to take away line and invite her to hit her favorite shot. Then I positioned our best floor defender, Sandy Scholtens, in the very spot Sarah liked to hit the ball. By the end of the match, Sandy had 29 digs, Sarah's hitting efficiency was a lowly (for her) .188, and we ran deliriously out of the gym with a 3-1 upset win. We had undermined Western Michigan's confidence by successfully defending against one of their best offensive players. And we did it by tactically manipulating the position of our block in an effort to channel the attack into a predictable area.

Control Blocking

So far I have talked about the block as having two tactical purposes. The first is to stuff the ball back into the opponent's court for a point or a side-out. The second is to position the block in a predetermined area and channel the attack into a specific zone in the defensive court. One result of both of these tactics is the control block. In a control block, the ball is deflected high off the blocker's hands, thereby enabling one of the backcourt defenders to play an easy free ball to the setter. Seen in this sense, a control block is a sometimes unintentional but always acceptable result of a stuff or channel tactic.

The control block can also be intentional. In control blocking, sometimes called soft blocking, the wrists are cocked backward and, with palms up, the blocker intentionally tries to deflect the attack high into the air on his or her own side of the net, thereby creating an easy free-ball reception for a teammate. This style of blocking is often recommended for players who cannot jump high enough to execute the net penetration required for stuff blocking, or who cannot get high enough over the net to take away enough court to channel effectively. Intentional or not, control blocking plays a major role in the effectiveness of any defense.

Adjusting the Block to the Depth of the Set

The line-versus-crosscourt-positioning concepts addressed so far assume the set (the point at which the hitter's hand contacts the ball) to be of normal depth, approximately 12 to 30 inches from the net. Should the set be of abnormal depth (closer than 12 inches or further than 30 inches), blockers must adjust their set-up positions in order to take away the same court area. Figure 3.2 illustrates the principle that, in setting up a block crosscourt, for example, the farther off the net the set location, the farther inside the outside blocker must set up.

When a set is tight to the net (closer than 12 inches), blockers should abandon all channeling or area blocking tactics, position their feet at the

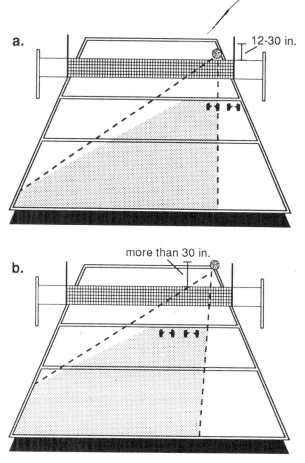

Figure 3.2 Adjusting the block against a deep set in order to protect same crosscourt angle: location of block against normal set depth (12-30 in. off net) (a), location of block against deep set (off net) more than 30 in. (b).

point of attack, and penetrate with both hands in an attempt to stuff the ball. The straight down attack angle made possible by the tight set usually spells disaster when a crosscourt blocker fails to make this adjustment. I refer to this as the "tight set rule," and when a tight set is spotted, it supersedes any other blocking tactic.

Tactical Blocking Concepts

In addition to choosing where and how to position the blockers in relation to the point of attack, a coach must also design a tactical system of blocking. The location decisions made by each of the three blockers must be consistent with an overall blocking philosophy. The following are some of the fundamental concepts which must be addressed when planning a system of blocking.

Read Versus Commit Blocking

Prior to the evolution of the quick attack, it was sufficient to read block against any set. Read blocking means that the blockers watch (i.e., read) the setter, wait until the set is made, and then move to block at the point of attack. If a team reads correctly, they should have at least two blockers on almost every set. This system is very effective against second tempo and high sets, but less effective against the quick set. The better the quick attack, meaning the quicker the timing and the higher the spiker's contact point, the greater the probability that it will beat a read blocking system.

Commit blocking evolved to solve this problem. Commit blocking means that the blockers, usually one or two designated blockers in the system, jump *with* the quick hitter. This enables the commit blocker to be in the air with the quick hitter and in a position to block the quick attack. Commit blocking usually discourages an opponent's intent to run a quick offense.

Of course, the disadvantage of the commit system is that if the setter sets away from the quick option—unless the set is very high, thereby allowing the commit blocker to land, recover, and move laterally to form a double block—the middle blocker will be out of the play and there will be only one blocker at the point of attack. A good setter will recognize the commit tactic and set to a second or third option hoping to get the one-on-one situation.

One of the dilemmas in preparing to defend against a team capable of running an effective, quick offense is whether to use a read or a commit blocking system. Nothing illustrates this dilemma more clearly than deciding how to block against the popular, right-side "X" play. If well executed, the play sends a quick hitter in front of the setter to attack a 1 set. The right-side hitter runs diagonally from right to left, crossing behind the quick hitter, to attack a 2 set (see Figure 3.3). If executed correctly by the setter, the quick hitter gets the ball when the defense is in a read-block mode, and the second-option hitter gets the ball when the defense is in a commit-block mode. The block is always at a disadvantage. The read blockers are still on the ground as the quick hitter is being set, and the commit blockers are descending from their jumps as the second-option hitter is ascending to attack.

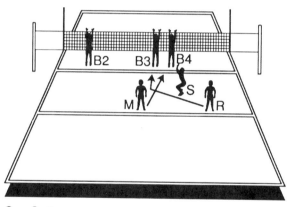

S = Setter
M = Middle hitter
R = Right-side (second-option) hitter
B = Blockers

Figure 3.3 Blocking the X play.

Only top level international and collegiate teams execute the quick attack effectively enough to warrant a decision to commit block. Most coaches rely on read blocking to stop combination attack patterns, such as the X play. They feel that their read blockers will be in good position to stop the second option and can get their hands up fast enough at least to control block against the quick set.

Stack Blocking

In addition to the commit versus read problem, defending against the X play also forces a second issue. Should blockers B4 and B3 (in Figure 3.3) deploy a strict man-to-man concept with B4 assigned to R and B3 assigned to M, thereby requiring B4 to cross behind B3 in order to get a block on R? Or should B4 and B3 use a switching system, similar to a matchup zone in basketball or a zone pass defense in football, so that B4 takes M and B3 switches over to take R on the crossing pattern? For years the latter has been preferred. But even though top level blockers have become skilled at communicating when they release a hitter to another zone and at looking for crossing patterns coming into their own zones, the quicker the offense, the greater the probability that it could beat a switch block to the point of attack.

As offenses continued to develop, they exposed yet a third major deficiency in the prevailing blocking tactics. Offenses were becoming more efficient at getting the ball to the best attacker, using different set tempos and different attack zones. Blocking systems were inflexible in the sense that there was no built-in mechanism for matching up the best blocker against the best hitter. If the hitter ran out of the best blocker's zone, the blocker was frozen out of the play, and the hitter was free to swing against a weaker block. Setting a good hitter against a weak blocker became a primary offensive tactic, and for years, blocking tactics lagged behind, unable to find a suitable solution.

By the end of the 1970s, blockers at the higher levels of play were facing these same three problems: when to commit versus when to read; when to go one-on-one versus when to switch; and how to match blocking strength against attack strength. Again it was the innovative USA Men's National Team staff that developed and popularized a tactical answer to these dilemmas. They created what has come to be known as stack blocking.

Stack blocking combines the commit with the read mode and man-to-man with zone, and is motivated by two principles. First, it is designed to stop the quick attack and still have the ability to get two blockers up against higher sets. And second, it provides the flexibility necessary to allow the best blocker to go up against the opponent's strongest hitter.

A stack-blocking alignment always assigns one blocker to jump with (i.e., commit to) the opponent's quick hitter. Another blocker, the stack blocker, lines up just behind the commit blocker (see Figure 3.4). The stack blocker's assignment is to read the set and go to the point of attack (this is identical to the responsibility of the middle blocker in the orthodox, read-blocking system). The remaining blocker functions normally as an outside blocker opposite the stack blocker. If the opponent sets the ball in Area 2 or 3, the stack blocker moves to block at the point of attack and is joined, when possible, by the commit blocker, who has descended from the jump against the quick set. If the opponent sets Area 4, the stack blocker moves laterally to join the outside blocker in a double block. There are two clear advantages to this system. First, there is always a good block up against the quick attack without the threat of sacrificing a double block against high sets to Area 4. And second, by assigning blockers

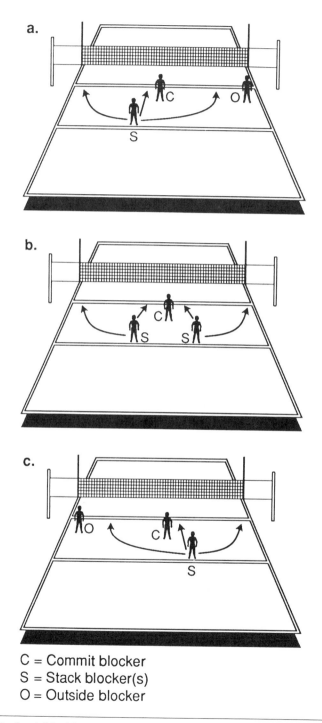

C = Commit blocker
S = Stack blocker(s)
O = Outside blocker

Figure 3.4 Stack blocking: stack left (a), double stack (b), stack right (c).

to specific roles in the system, the coach can match the best blocker against the opponent's top hitter. If this is the quick hitter, for example, the best blocker can be assigned to the commit position. If the top hitter is a high set attacker, then the best blocker should be in the stack position, able to chase the high set no matter which way it goes. Against a versatile attack player capable of hitting both high and quick sets, the primary blocker can be assigned a dual role, laying back in the stack position, but ready to jump as a commit blocker if the hitter goes quick.

It is important to point out that stack blocking is not the same as orthodox, one-on-one blocking. The purpose of stack blocking is still to get at least two blockers to the point of attack. In this sense, it is identical to read blocking. It is true that an efficient, quick offense will create the same problems for the stack system that it creates for the read system; that is, because one blocker always commits with the quick option, it is sometimes difficult for the commit blocker to recover and go up against second tempo sets. But the stack system represents a significant tactical step forward over the read system in that it has been much more successful in addressing the commit versus read issue, the problem of when to switch in the zone concept, and how to match up blocking strength against attacking strength.

However, I'd like to stress that for most levels of play, the read system is the preferred blocking alignment. First, it involves no difficult-to-execute lateral move by a blocker from an off-net stack position to an outside set-up position. And second, very few levels of play feature a quick attack of such efficiency that it would consistently beat a read blocker.

Remember, the strength of the read block system is that there will always be a good chance of having two or more blockers at the point of attack. The only reason for moving to the more advanced and more difficult stack system is because efficient offensive execution by the opponent would require it.

Release Blocking

A popular tactic over the last several years has been to release block against selected offensive situations. Release blocking means that the middle blocker in a normal read block system releases early to form a double block at an anticipated point of attack. The most common release block situation occurs when the opponent's setter is in a front row rotational position and the two front row attackers approach to hit in front of the setter. For example, if the offensive team is lined up in a stack-left receiving formation (see Figure 3.5), the middle blocker (B3) reads attacker M. If M moves to attack in front of the setter, B3 releases early to join B2 in a double team against L, and B4 moves inside to block against M and the possibility of a second-contact attack by the setter, I would

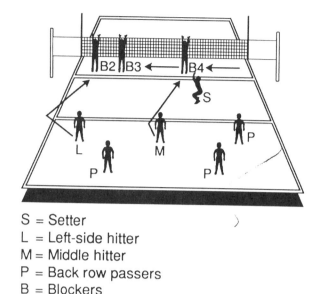

S = Setter
L = Left-side hitter
M = Middle hitter
P = Back row passers
B = Blockers

Figure 3.5 Release blocking versus stack-left receiving. *Note*: A stack-left formation means that the two eligible front row attackers (M and L) are stacked on the left side of the receiving pattern.

suggest that B4 commit block against an in-system pass. Even if the offensive team lines up in another formation, such as a stack-right or a split configuration (see Figure 3.6), B3 reads the approach patterns of the attackers, and if both move to attack in front of the setter, then B3 releases to join B2 on the outside.

If, in any of these front row–setter offensive formations, one attacker approaches to attack behind the setter and the other in front of the setter, then the blocking team remains in a standard, read-block format. And, of course, if both attackers move to attack behind the setter, then the release block principle would apply in reverse. That is, B3 would release to join B4 on the outside, and B2 would move inside to take the middle attacker.

Two additional points can be made about release blocking. First, it is motivated by the idea that there is a defensive advantage to be gained by getting the middle blocker outside early to execute a solid, double block against the opponent's outside hitter. This is sound reasoning in most instances. One exception occurs, however, when the opponent's M (in Figure 3.5) is their primary hitter. It would probably be wiser to keep B3 inside to guard against the set to M before releasing to block with B2 against the high outside set to L. Second, bad-pass releasing can apply any time an inaccurate pass puts the setter in a situation when he

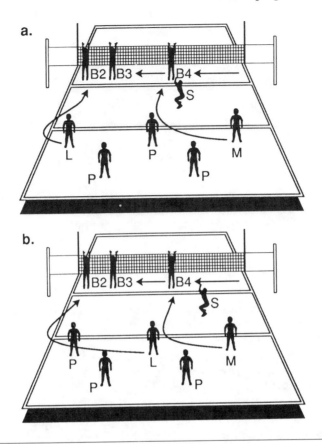

Figure 3.6 Release blocking versus split (a) and stack-right (b) receiving formations.

or she is in an obvious high outside set situation. Blocker B3 can release early to whichever side the outside hitter is deployed.

Release blocking remains very popular among teams at all levels of play. But this tactic is being countered by use of the back row attack. As the back row attack capabilities of teams increase, the tactical advantages of release blocking will decrease. Figure 3.7 illustrates how the threat of setting the C to the back row hitter in Position 1 can force B4 to "stay at home" and thereby nullify any opportunity for B3 to release from blocking responsibilities against M.

Base Position and Switching Options

Base position for blockers is the formation in which the three blockers wait as they prepare to react to the opponent's attack. The most popular

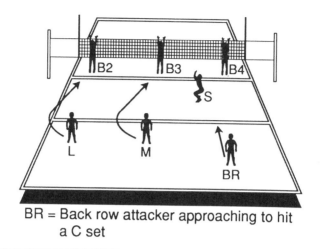

BR = Back row attacker approaching to hit a C set

Figure 3.7 Back row attack as a counter to release blocking.

formation (see Figure 3.8), used by most coaches of women's collegiate and junior club teams, deploys blockers in an unbalanced configuration. The left-side blocker (B4) is approximately 10 feet from the left sideline, the middle blocker (B3) is equidistant from either sideline, and the right-side blocker (B2) is approximately 4 feet from the right sideline.

Blocker B2 read-blocks anything coming to an outside zone to L. Some teams prefer to ask B2 to start farther inside to help against a possible 3 set. Blocker B3 must be prepared to go up against all quick sets in the middle zones, as well as to move laterally to form a double block against higher sets to the outside zones. Blocker B4 starts close to B3 in order to help read-block against a possible quick set, yet must move to block against a high set to R. This inside base position by B4 is a result of a

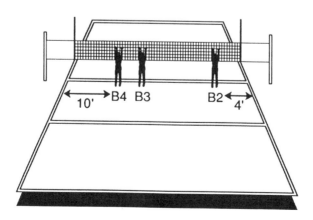

Figure 3.8 Unbalanced sample base positions for blockers.

tactical consensus among most coaches that (1) it is difficult for only one blocker (e.g., B3) to stop an effective quick attack, and (2) most teams do not execute the back set to R with great frequency or effectiveness. Blocker B4's position near B3 in the unbalanced base position scheme is seen as a way to increase the chances of a successful block against either eventuality. Of course, against a team possessing a strong right-side attack this particular configuration could become a liability and would have to be abandoned and B4 moved closer to the left sideline.

I would add an additional note to the base position of B2. Some coaches like to start this blocker approximately 3 feet off the net and turned at a 45 degree angle toward the opponent's setter. This allows B2 to defend against the setter attack, to be in a good position to pick up the quick attack "tip," and to play deflections along the net, yet still be able to move into blocking position against the high left-side attack from L. Recently I have seen more and more teams make this adjustment.

Common Base Position Options

At the higher levels of play—men's and women's international and men's collegiate levels—two base position options are common. One, the stack alignment, has already been discussed. This base position, with one or two players lined up further off the net than the middle blocker, is used when teams are in a commit-block mode.

In situations where a team is in a standard, read-block mode, blockers are in balanced, evenly spaced base positions along the net with all three blockers compressed toward the center of the court (see Figure 3.9). Two concepts motivate this base position tactic. First, because the middle zones can be attacked with such suddenness and quickness, they must be protected by having both outside blockers start inside and ready to

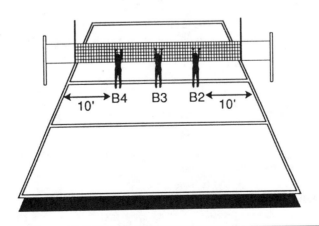

Figure 3.9 Balanced sample base positions for blockers.

help B3. Second, top level teams all have deceptive setters, who are capable of using all available front and back row attackers to hit any type of set in any zone. Forced to guard against all attack options, all three blockers must wait in a balanced, neutral position and be ready to read-block against whatever attack sequence develops. Any attempt to unbalance the block base position, as in the earlier example, would invite the opponent's setter to attack the open areas created by the imbalance.

Until recently, most teams deployed their blockers in base formation according to position. If you were a middle blocker, you lined up in the middle base position, left-side blockers on the left, and right-side blockers on the right. Two concepts have evolved to soften this strict adherence to positional discipline. One concept, already mentioned, is the stack-block scheme with its emphasis on matching the best blockers against the opponent's best hitters. The second concept is switching.

Switching involves reassigning blockers away from their normal positions in the base configuration in an attempt to gain a desired matchup with a particular hitter. Once the blockers are switched and in place, they function in a normal read-block fashion, without the commit-block option present in the stack scheme.

Let me give you a brief example. Many teams possess only one or two players with exceptional attack skills. It is no secret that these players will receive the majority of the sets in that team's offensive system. It can be extremely effective to switch your best blocker to line up opposite the opponent's priority hitters. This might mean that your middle blocker will have to line up in base position as the right-side blocker or the left-side blocker. The advantage is that you will have your best blocker squared off against your opponent's best hitter. But there are two disadvantages. First, your blocking capabilities will be diminished if they decide to set away from their priority attacker. And second, transition offense can be a bit tricky if your team digs a ball and, for example, your setter has switched to block on the left and is now your outside hitter, and your middle hitter has switched to block on the right and now must execute setting responsibilities. Nevertheless, block switching in base position to gain desirable matchups has become an extremely popular tactic.

Base Deception

Most coaches feel that it is important to show the same base position, whatever that base position may be, before each defensive opportunity. Linebackers in football, for example, show the same base position at the outset of each play even though on one down they have pass-rush responsibilities, and on the next down they are assigned to drop into the secondary for pass coverage. In the same fashion, B4 may be assigned to commit with B3 against a 1 set to M and, on the next play, be asked to split out early to guard against the 9 set to R. By lining up in the same base position both times, the opponent is not alerted to B4's intentions prior to the blocking sequence. Using the same base position, therefore, serves to mask the tactical intent of the block.

At the same time, I have always been intrigued by the notion of base deception. This tactic would call for blockers to line up differently, both individually and as a team, before each defensive opportunity. Using the previous example, B4 might take an inside base position when the early split-out tactic was called, and perhaps take an outside base position when intending to help inside against the 1. On the next sequence, the base positions could be reversed, and on the next sequence, still another base position could be used. The object here would be to confuse the opponent with multiple and deceptive base position configurations. I have tried this from time to time with my teams at Illinois. Against those well-coached teams whose players are trained to consider an opponent's base position in deciding where to direct their attack, it has at least served as a distraction to them. Of course, against teams who remain oblivious to their opponent's base position tactics, base deception "falls on deaf ears."

FLOOR DEFENSE

If the attack gets by the block, floor defenders must be in position to dig the ball. The exact location for each defender depends on the position of the block in relation to the attack and on the specific defensive philosophy employed by the coach. It is the coordination of blocking tactics and the corresponding configuration of floor defenders that constitutes a defensive scheme.

Base Position

The unpredictability of the opponent's attack requires a balanced base position for floor defenders. Not only must the ready posture of each defender be balanced, but the configuration of the three back row defenders on the floor must also be balanced before the attack develops. This balanced base position combines preparedness to defend against any first- or second-contact attack, against any third-contact quick attack, and against all high set attacks.

The following example (see Figure 3.10) outlines one of the popular formats for a defensive base position scheme. Blockers B4, B3, and B2 are aligned as they appear in Figure 3.8. The player in Position 1 is

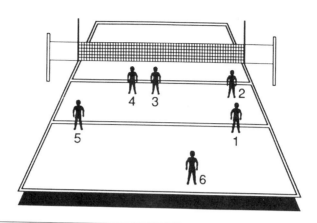

Figure 3.10 Defensive base position.

approximately 4 to 5 feet from the right sideline, at a 45 degree angle facing the opponent's setter. If the opponent's setter is in the front row, Player 1 shortens up a base position at or within 6 to 12 inches of the 3-meter line. This allows Player 1 to be in good position to dig the setter attack. If the opponent's setter is in the back row and, therefore, no second-contact setter attack is likely, Player 1 drops back to a location 3 to 4 feet from the attack line. In either location, Player 1 must also hold and be prepared to dig any third-contact quick attack. Player 6 lines up approximately 6 to 8 feet from the baseline and just to the right of center. This right-of-center position allows Player 6 to be in a high activity area for digging quick sets, especially the 3 set. And Player 5 occupies the same setter-dump, quick attack area as Player 1, but on the opposite side of the court. It is from this base position that the team defends against the variety of attack options it will have to face.

It is important that you understand: When designing a base position, a coach's choice of which areas of the court to protect must be the result of a logical thought process. You must analyze the attack tendencies of the teams you play and design a base position that makes sense for your level. The base position I have described is one I have used for years. But there have been occasions when it had to be reevaluated and changed. Let met give you an example.

In 1987, we drew the University of Pittsburgh as our first-round NCAA tournament opponent. After watching videotapes of their team, I noticed that their two middle hitters liked (or were trained) to attack 1 sets, deep to the corners. Neither one of them hit the ball very hard, but their ability to hit the corners had made them effective. Our customary base position would have been a poor one for defending against this particular shot. I

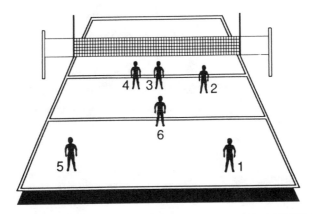

Figure 3.11 Adjusted base position.

adjusted out alignment so that we would have two defenders guarding the corners (see Figure 3.11) and only one player protecting the short zone. It worked marvelously, and it was one of the reasons we walked away with a 3-1 victory.

Base-to-Read Movement

Whenever an opponent sets the ball high (a 2 set, or higher), the defensive team has time to read the point of attack and organize into a specific defensive alignment. The elapsed time between the initial contact by the setter and the contact by the hitter is very short—anywhere from 1.5 to 3 seconds. But within this brief span of time, the defensive team can move quickly from its base position to its read position in the defensive scheme being deployed.

Figure 3.12 depicts the base-to-read movement patterns for each player using the popular rotation defense against an attack from Area 4. Because the time available for executing these movements is so short, it is critical that efficient footwork patterns be designed for each position. Players 4 and 5 have particularly difficult assignments. They must move anywhere from 10 to 14 feet away from the net, turn around and stop in a balanced, forward position, and all while staying focused on the relevant cues as to what type of shot might be coming their way. This requires absolute efficiency of movement by each defender, and it can be achieved only through many hours of practice. Therefore, repetitions of base-to-read movement patterns ought to be a staple in every coach's practice plan.

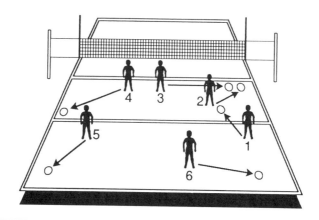

Figure 3.12 Base-to-read movement rotation defense.

Read Sequencing

As the opponents circulate the ball in their system of attack, each player on the defensive team, fixed in their defensive base positions, begins a sequence of reads. These reads provide the information necessary for players to decide which movement patterns to execute in each defensive situation. Using Figure 3.12, let's look at the sequencing responsibilities normally assigned to Player 5 in a rotation defense.

After determining whether the opposing team is in a back or front row–setter rotation, and thereby knowing whether or not to be concerned about a second-contact dump by the setter, the left-back player's first responsibility is to guard against the possible overpass, that is, the opponent's sending the ball back over the net on the first contact. Next, if the opponent's setter is in a front row rotation, the setter attack must be anticipated and defended. If there is no setter attack, Player 5 then moves to defend against the next possible attack in the sequence—the quick attack to the seam between Areas 4 and 5. Player 5 must also be ready to chase down any tips put over or around the block by the quick hitter.

If none of these options is selected, it can be deduced safely that the ball will be set high (second tempo or higher). This means that the defender in Position 5 will have time to move out of base position into a read position relative to the location of the high set. If the opponent sets a 2, Player 5 will stay close to Area 4 to guard against the tip around the block. If they set a 5, Player 5 must retreat quickly toward the sideline to dig the inside crosscourt angle left open by the block. If the opponent sets a 9, Player 5 holds in base position to cover the tip over the block.

In each instance, once a player moves to his or her initial read position in the defensive system, a final read is made to establish the optimum digging position. This final read is influenced by a number of factors. First, the defender must assess the disposition of the block. Is it tightly formed? Is there a hole between the two blockers? Where is the block set up along the line-versus-crosscourt spectrum? Second, the defender must evaluate the body position of the attacker in relation to the depth of the set and the location of the block. Has the attacker overrun the set and is, therefore, in a bad position to hit a sharp, downward angle? Has the setter trapped the hitter into the block (a trap set is a set tight to the net, which leaves the attacker without enough room to take a good swing at the ball), making a tip or a wipeoff the only possible shots? Has the hitter planted improperly, leaving the set too far right or left and thereby cutting down on the variety of possible angles of attack? Has the set travelled past the antenna, leaving only a limited angle within which the attacker can direct the ball?

Within 1 to 3 seconds, the defender must process all of this information, make a final read on the play, and get into the optimum position for digging the ball. Each position has its own sequencing requirements, and each player must make the correct reads if the full defense is to function in an efficient fashion.

Basic Defensive Alignments

Though I am a devout advocate of the notion that creativity, innovation, and specialization should guide a coach in designing defenses to meet specific situations, I also agree that certain standard defenses, which have significant tactical merit, have evolved over the years. I would like to review a few of these basic defensive alignments. In each case, I will describe the positioning patterns for defending against the high set attack from the opponent's Area 4. To defend against the high set attack from Area 2, simply reverse the position patterns.

Perimeter Defense

The first alignment is the perimeter defense (see Figure 3.13). The perimeter defense is designed to provide maximum coverage against the hard-driven spike. Four backcourt defenders (Players 4, 5, 6, and 1) are situated around two blockers (3 and 2), each in a perimeter position near a sideline or baseline. The unprotected area of the court is the middle, leaving this defensive scheme vulnerable to the tip and off-speed shot deep into Area 3 or shallow into Area 6.

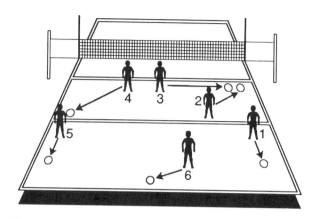

Figure 3.13 Perimeter defense.

Rotation Defense

The second is the rotation defense (illustrated previously in Figure 3.12). The rotation defense combines two strengths. First, it assigns one player to cover the tip and off-speed shot (Player 1). Second, it protects against the deep corner attack (Players 5 and 6). Its vulnerabilities lie in assigning only three backcourt defenders (Players 4, 5, and 6) to dig the hard-driven spike, and in having no player assigned to defend Area 6. As the ball is set high to Area 4, all four nonblockers (Players 4, 5, 6, and 1) rotate around the perimeter of the court toward the point of attack—thus, the name *rotation* defense.

Slide Defense

The third is the slide defense (see Figure 3.14). This defense combines the tip coverage of rotation defense with the middle-back protection of perimeter defense. The offside blocker (Player 4) slides toward the point of attack to play tips and deflections, hence the name *slide* defense. Its weakness is using only three backcourt defenders and leaving the corners unprotected against hard-driven spikes. It is also vulnerable to the tip over the block into Area 1 near the sideline and Area 4.

Situational Defensive Reads

Base position tactics provide the structure for defending against the first or second contact and against the quick attack on the third contact. The

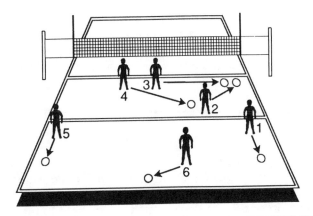

Figure 3.14 Slide defense.

basic defensive alignments provide tactical positioning assignments against the orthodox high sets to Areas 4 and 2. But there are a variety of situations that arise in the course of a match that do not fall into any of these categories, yet require a well-rehearsed defensive response.

Split Block

One goal of any defense is to have two players take away an area of the court by forming a tight, well-positioned double block at the point of attack. A tight block means that there are no seams or holes in the block, forcing the attacker to hit around or over the block. If the floor defenders are positioned correctly, there is a good chance that the ball will be dug. But if the block is not well formed as a result of poor technique or inability of the middle blocker to close to the outside quickly enough, or because the opponent's offensive tactics have forced a blocker out of position, the integrity of the defensive system breaks down.

When the problem is poor execution by individual blockers, such as positioning hands improperly, drifting past the point of attack, batting at the ball with the wrists, mistiming the play or opening a seam between the hands, floor defenders are placed at a severe disadvantage. It becomes more difficult for floor defenders to anticipate the angle of attack. Unpredictable deflections off the blocker's hands are more likely. The defensive confidence inspired by clear reads around a solid, tight block gives way to frustration and panic. The only solution at this point is to go back to the practice gym and review the fundamentals of blocking.

But even teams with decent blocking technique frequently face the problem of having to play defense behind a split block or behind only one blocker. These situations usually occur when the middle blocker must hold position in the center of the net to guard against a possible quick attack and then release to the outside to form a double block against the high set to Area 4 or 2. When the middle blocker does not make it to the outside in time, either because of lack of speed or because of the swiftness of the opponent's outside set, the floor defenders must read the situation and adjust their positions to play behind a split block or only one blocker at the point of attack.

Figure 3.15 illustrates how each of the defenses described above would adjust to the split block situation. In the rotation defense, Player 5 moves into the area left open by the hole in the block. In the slide and perimeter defenses, this adjustment is made by Player 6. In all cases, the depth of the read (how deep or shallow the digger is positioned within the attack angle) depends on the distance of the set from the net and on the position of the attacker in relation to the set. If the set is tight to the net and the hitter is in perfect position to execute a hard swing, then the defender must move to a shallow digging position. If the set is off the net and the hitter, for example, has run too far under the ball, then the attack trajectory will be deep and the defender should be positioned accordingly. All other players in the defensive scheme should maintain their original reads. Only the player assigned to play behind the block should be on the lookout for the split block situation and be prepared to make a significant adjustment.

High Set Attack From Area 3

Though most teams prefer to use quick sets to attack the middle of the net, others like to use a higher set (second tempo or higher). This is usually accomplished by sending a combination hitter into the middle to attack a 2 set off the quick hitter's 3, 1, or 6 set. Sometimes, however, there is no attempt to deceive the block with a combination sequence. Some teams simply like to set a high ball in the middle. They prefer the lower risk of the high set. And they feel that the attack angles and tip opportunities afforded by the high, middle set are difficult to defend.

In either case, whether a second tempo, combination set or an isolated, high set to a middle attacker, the high set to Area 3 should be defended against in an organized fashion. Figure 3.16 illustrates the three options for designing a defensive scheme.

If a two-blocker scheme is preferred, then the blocking assignments can be determined by the location of the pass. If the pass is accurate and the opponent's setter is delivering the high, middle set from the normal position, Player 4 joins Player 3 to set a double block against the attacker. Player 5 moves up toward Area 4 to cover the tip. Player 2 moves off the net to cover the tip into Area 2. Player 1 reads the crosscourt attack angle. And Player 6 moves left or right along the baseline, depending on the

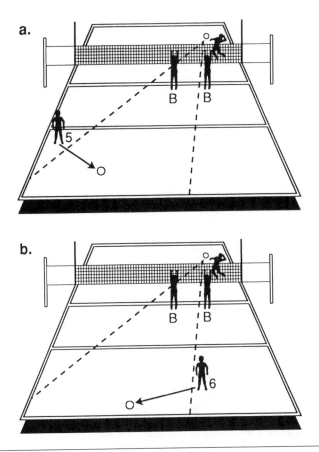

Figure 3.15 Defense behind split block in rotation defense (a) and slide or perimeter defense (b).

shoulder position of the hitter, and takes a position in the seam between the two blockers.

However, if the pass brings the opponent's setter beyond the midline of the court (toward the opponent's Area 4), the high set will be close to Player 2's blocking zone, and Player 2 should join Player 3 to form the block. In this case, the defensive assignments are reversed. Player 1 moves forward to cover the tip, and Player 5 digs the crosscourt angle. Player 4 stays to cover the tip into Area 4. Player 6 executes the same seam read.

On occasion it is effective to put up a triple block against this set. This would normally be when the pass is near the midline of the court. Player 2 would trigger this defensive option by moving inside to block with Players 3 and 4. Player 1 would read Player 2's movement and come up

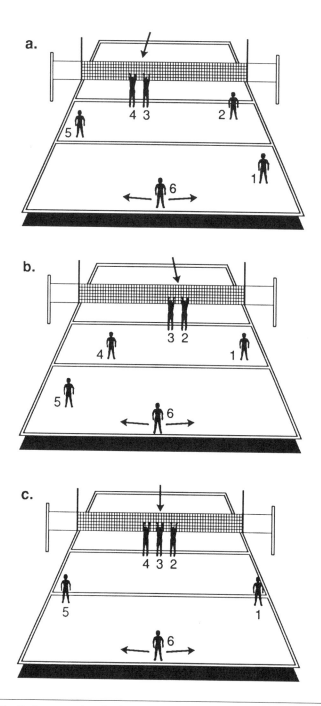

Figure 3.16 Defense against high set to Area 3: two blockers versus orthodox set origination (a), two blockers versus pass beyond midline (b), and three blockers (c).

the line to Area 2 to cover the tip. Player 5 makes the same move to cover the tip into Area 4. And Player 6 again roams the baseline, attempting to read the hitter's attack angle. Using three blockers is risky, in my opinion—it leaves too much court open in the event the ball is not blocked—and should only be used as a surprise element to keep the hitter off balance.

I'd like to make one final point about this defense. Ordinarily, when defending against the combination 2 set (for example, in the 1-2 combination crossing pattern), it is important that Players 4 and 3 stay together, executing a read block against both the 1 and the 2 sets. If either blocker commits against the 1 set, they will not be in position to form a double block against the 2, and the integrity of the defense will break down.

Inside Block Set-Up

In designing defenses against high sets to Areas 2 and 4, the positioning of players is based on the assumption that the set will travel all the way to the antenna, or at least within 1 meter of the antenna. From this set location, the hitter is able to choose from all possible attack angles, ranging from a shot straight down the line to a radical crosscourt angle. But frequently, either by design or because the setter has failed to push the set out far enough, the set falls short of the 1-meter, outside set zone. In this case, when the point of attack is more than 1 meter inside the antenna, a specific defensive adjustment must take place.

Figure 3.17 shows how the position of the set takes away the line option from the hitter attacking from Area 4. As the block moves inside to stay with the hitter, the amount of court available down the line is sealed off, and the hard shot down the line becomes virtually impossible. The hitter's only options are to attack crosscourt inside the block, hit hard off the block, or tip around the block. One of the popular shots in this situation is to tip back to the opponent's Area 2. In a rotation defense, this tip is automatically covered by Player 1, who rotates up under the block. But in the perimeter and slide defenses, Player 1 must release from the normal deep, line-digging position (remember, the hard, line shot has been taken away by the inside set location) and move quickly to Area 2 to await the tip. The same adjustment must be made against inside sets from the opponent's right side, except that the defensive roles are mirrored, because the attack comes from the opposite corner of the net.

The adjustment has come to be known as the inside set rule. If you are a line digger, responsible for a deep drop to defend the line shot, and the blockers in front of you move inside (more than 1 meter), you must rush forward to guard against the short tip toward the sideline. Teams at all levels continue to be burned by this tip, so this adjustment should be a fundamental part of any defensive system.

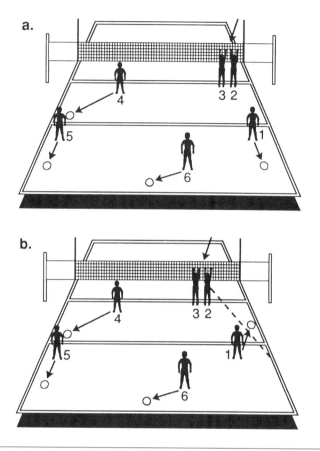

Figure 3.17 Defensive adjustment for inside block set-up: normal perimeter position for Player 1 (a), inside block adjustment for Player 1 (b).

Ball Outside Antenna

Because of the angles established by the configuration of the sideline, net, and antenna, any set that travels past the antenna creates a limited opportunity for the attacker. Figure 3.18 illustrates how the available attack angles become narrowed. The area of court open to the hitter is smaller (remember that the ball cannot legally strike the antenna). The farther past the antenna the set travels, the smaller the area of court available.

This circumstance requires a specific defensive adjustment (see Figure 3.18). First, B2 must position his or her outside hand adjacent to the antenna to prevent the ball from being hit into the space between the block and the antenna. The middle blocker, B3, closes to form a double

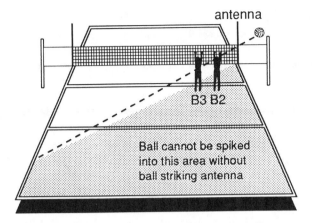

Figure 3.18 Ball outside antenna.

block. Because there is no chance that the ball can be spiked vertically down the line, both blockers should position their hands slightly farther apart, perhaps 8 to 10 inches, than they would against the normal attack situation, in which the distance between their hands would measure only 4 to 6 inches. As a result, the block ends up taking away more court, limiting the area for which floor defenders must be responsible when guarding against the high velocity spike. The player in Position 4 (in a rotation or perimeter defense) or Position 5 (in a slide defense) moves to dig in the crosscourt attack angle dictated by the depth and location of the set in relation to the antenna. Player 5 (in rotation) or Player 6 (in perimeter or slide) digs the seam of the block.

And finally, it is important that at least one player on the right side of the defense holds position to guard against deflections off the block—a common occurrence in this situation because of the severe attack angle and the position of the blocker's hands. As the hitter swings into the crosscourt angle, the ball can hit the side of a blocker's hand and rebound into Area 1 or 2 or perhaps into the adjacent out-of-bounds area. In the rotation defense, Player 1 moves inside to cover the tip, and Player 6 shifts all the way to the line to play these deflections. In the slide defense, Player 4 comes across to cover the tip, and Player 1 holds for deflections. Player 1 has the same assignment in the perimeter defense.

Back Row Attack

The first question to address when considering how to defend against the back row attack is whether or not to block. At most levels of play, the attack from the back row does not have enough velocity to warrant putting up a block. The chances of blocking the ball, measured against the possibility that the block might deflect the shot into an unretrievable area of the court, should be weighed carefully. It might be wiser to position floor defenders in a balanced perimeter position and try to dig the ball.

At the higher levels of play, however, the ball can be attacked with increased velocity and must be challenged by the block. Blocking tactics in this situation are identical to those applied against the front row attack, except that blockers often delay their jumps to compensate for the greater distance the ball must travel before it reaches the plane of the net. The configuration of floor defenders, however, should be modified (see Figure 3.19).

The three back row floor defenders must retreat to a deep position in the court, because it is unlikely that the ball can be hit with a sharp

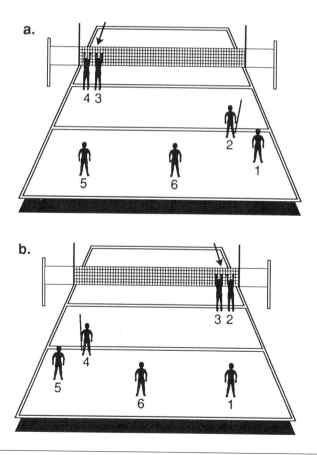

Figure 3.19 Defense versus back row attack: attack from Area 1 (a), attack from Area 5 (b).

downward angle. The offside blocker (the blocker farthest from the point of attack) drops to a position just beyond the attack line to guard against tips and deflections. And finally, the line of defense formed by the three deep receivers should be rotated or tilted slightly toward the point of attack. This ensures that the defense is balanced in relation to the attack angles.

Free Ball Reception

Often an opponent is unable to control the ball with enough efficiency to mount a successful attack and is forced by circumstance to send over the net a safe, low velocity ball, which is easily playable by the defense. When this occurs, it is called a free ball. It is important that your defensive scheme include a plan for how to receive free balls.

First, your team must develop good, free-ball recognition skills. While in base position, your players must evaluate the circulation of the ball by the opponent. Once the defensive players determine that it will be impossible for the opponent to generate an orthodox attack—the coach decides whether all or only designated players are assigned these recognition responsibilities—"free ball" is called out. This is the signal for the defensive team to move into free-ball reception position.

There are numerous free-ball reception theories. Here is the one I have used for many years and consider the most practical and effective (Figure 3.20). First, I prefer that my middle blocker stay at the net, prepared to block. She is to jump to block only if she is 100% certain that she will stuff the ball back into the opponent's court. Otherwise, I prefer that she stay down and allow one of the floor defenders to pass the ball. Remember, this is a free ball, and I don't want a blocker deflecting the ball into difficult areas of the court. When she stays down, I also want her to hold her position adjacent to the net. By backing up into the reception pattern, she can disrupt the reads by the back row defenders. As soon as the pass is executed, the middle blocker can release from the net and move into her counterattack pattern.

In front row–setter rotations, the setter (Player 2) is already in position at the net to receive the pass. Player 1 holds in her base position. Player 4 moves off the net to a wing position just behind the attack line. Players 5 and 6 move into a balanced, two-player receiving tandem 20 to 22 feet deep in the court. These two players are responsible for receiving all free balls. I prefer the clarity of the two-person reception pattern over the confusion often generated by deploying multiple receivers. The two wing players are responsible for all soft shots or tips falling near the 3-meter line. Another advantage of the two-person pattern is that the front row attackers are virtually free from reception responsibilities and can concentrate on their attack assignments.

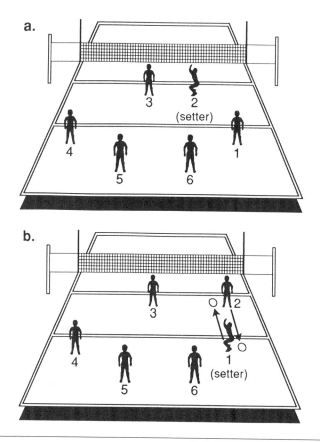

Figure 3.20 Free-ball reception with front row setter (a) and back row setter (b).

In the back row–setter rotations, the assignments on the right side of the defense are reversed. Upon hearing "free ball," the setter (Player 1) moves immediately to the net to receive the anticipated pass. Player 2 drops to the right-side wing position. Finally, Player 6 must move immediately to her right as the setter vacates Area 1. Many teams are trained to send free balls into Area 1 in an attempt to catch the defensive team executing this switch too slowly.

Tailoring Defense to Your Team's Needs

It is clear that the past few decades have yielded elaborate and complicated theories about how to defend against modern offensive systems. The problem for today's coach is how to digest the overwhelming volume of information and then design and teach a defensive system of play. The creative abilities of the coach must surface at this point.

A coach cannot simply memorize a defensive system and superimpose it on a team. The system ideas must be evaluated and tailored, not only to fit a team's particular abilities, but also to address the styles of offense that likely will be used by opponents. A series of questions a coach should ask are listed in the following box.

Questions to Ask When Tailoring a Defense

1. Do I have capable blockers in each position? If not, how do I cope with blocking liabilities?

2. What is the nature of the opponent's attack system? What percentage of spikes are down the line or crosscourt? Do they attack from the back row? Do they attack quick, or are they a high, outside team? What percentage of their attacks are tips or off-speed? Should we block against everyone, or do they have some attackers who are weak and inconsistent?

3. Do we have a weak block and so should play a four-back, perimeter defense? Or do we have a solid block, allowing us to play a three-back defense with one player covering the tip?

4. Where should I play my best defender? If we play rotation defense, do I block line and put my best defender in Position 5, in order to be in a high traffic area against the opponent's left-side attack? If we play a slide or perimeter defense, should I put my best defender in Position 6 for the same reason?

5. Do I want my players to specialize in the back row? Should my middle blockers always play middle-back, left-sides play left-back, and setter and right-side play right-back? Or should I allow for flexibility in positioning players in the backcourt?

6. Do I play the same defense all the time so that my players become proficient at one defense? Or do I teach different defenses to address different situations?

7. Do I want the same defense against the high, outside set to be played against sets from both Area 2 and Area 4? Or do I want to consider playing a rotation, for example, against Area 4 and a slide against Area 2? [This might be a wise approach if you coach a team with a slow setter, who would have difficulty getting from a defensive read position in Zone 1 (defending against an Area 2 attack) all the way to the net to run the transition offense. In a slide alignment, the setter would be much closer to the net, and the transition movement demands would be less.]

Wrap-Up

The coaches whose teams play good defense will be the coaches who not only become well schooled in a variety of system designs and approaches to technical training, but who also are able to apply this knowledge to maximize their teams' abilities.

Implications for Defensive Training

Having played or coached volleyball since 1962, I can tell you that no other area of the game has been subjected to such diverse and often conflicting theories of technique as has volleyball defense. We first learned to dig the ball with one arm while executing a shoulder roll. Later we were taught to do a sprawl while digging the ball with two arms. Then we were shown the side layout and barrel roll techniques. And all the while, there have been those who argued that no one can be called a good defensive player without knowing how to execute the dive.

Twenty years ago, it was considered sound to keep your weight back on the heels and cushion the ball with the platform and body. Technical experts later insisted that the weight should be forward and that the platform should extend away from the body and should drive under and through the ball. Some prefer that floor defenders take balanced, stationary positions as the hitter contacts the ball. Others, especially those who teach the pre-hop move, prefer that the defenders be in unbalanced, forward-lunging positions at contact.

A number of other issues have surfaced as well. In teaching defense, is it better to run high energy, rapid movement drills, which emphasize tempo? Or is it better to slow things down and insist on correct technique with every contact? Is it better to simulate gamelike conditions at all times and run drills that emphasize digging balls that are attacked with an approach from the other side of the net and with a block in place? Or can defense be learned in drills that feature a coach hitting balls from an ungamelike position on the floor and on the same side of the net as the defender?

I have wrestled through the years with these and many other issues surrounding volleyball defense and how to teach it. In the paragraphs that follow I will summarize for you those principles that I have found to be the most reliable and effective.

BLOCKING PRINCIPLES

I often feel that blocking is the hardest skill to teach. After all, a player can do everything correctly—from making the read on the hitter to executing the blocking technique—but, because the hitter tips the ball over the block, experience no tangible sign of success. According to my statistics, even if the hitter takes a normal swing, the block's chances of stuffing the ball are less than 10%. In other words, in a match in which the opponent accumulates 150 attack attempts, it would be unusual for your team to record more than 15 terminal stuff blocks (this is true at least at the women's collegiate level). The feedback is usually more positive for other skills. Spikers, for example, will record kills anywhere from 30 to 50% of the time. Passers are reasonably successful 80 to 90% of the time. Setters' success rates are even higher. The infrequency in positive feedback is one of the reasons blocking is so difficult to teach.

Successful blocking, therefore, must be measured not only by how many stuff blocks or control blocks a player records, but also by how much discipline the blocker exercises in setting the block, how accurately the blocker times the jump, how much court the blocker takes away, and how accurately the floor defenders are able to set up behind the block. Correct blocking technique requires the mastering of a complicated pattern of decision-making skills and precise movements that must be executed within a 1 to 3 second time frame.

Coiled Posture

Because the blocker does not know in advance where the opponent's setter is going to set the ball, the blocker must wait in base position and be prepared either to jump straight up or to move laterally to the left or right before jumping to block. For years I searched for an appropriate key word to describe the ''ready'' posture I thought necessary for blockers to maintain as they made their reads and prepared to execute their block.

In the mid-1980s, with the help of former assistant coach Don Hardin, I came upon the word *coiled*.

Blockers must be in a posture that allows them to explode quickly into their blocking move. There is no time to gather their balance, bend the knees, reach down and lift the arms upward while thrusting off the floor, and then reach to block the ball (this is especially true when guarding against the possibility of a quick attack before moving to block against a higher option). The blocker must already be in a posture that will allow the quickest possible reaction to the ball, whether it is a lateral move to close with an outside blocker or an explosive vertical move to block a quick attack. We decided that the word that most closely approximated this posture is the one that describes how a rattlesnake prepares to strike—coiled.

Coiled posture means that a blocker waits in base position as described in the box that follows.

Coiled Posture in Base Position

1. Knees are bent sufficiently so that only one move is required to explode upward or dart laterally from the base posture. Having to bend the knees deeper before jumping or moving laterally wastes precious fractions of a second.

2. Hands are held high, slightly above the head and about shoulder-width apart. This is critical when in a read-block mode protecting against the quick attack. The speed with which the blocker's hands move from the base position to the point of attack is obviously of paramount importance. It is absolutely mandatory that blockers not drop their hands in an attempt to jump. There is not enough time. The hands stay high and the thrust comes from the legs.

When teaching the coiled posture, it is important to stress that the coil must be sustained before and during the setter's contact with the ball. A common error is that blockers may stay in a tight, coiled position as the opponent passes the ball, but then lose their focus as they get caught up in watching hitters run their offensive patterns. For example, the knees lose their coil as the blocker's body elongates in anticipation of jumping to stop a quick attack. Then the setter pushes the ball to another hitter, and the blocker must regather in order to move to the actual point of attack. Coiled posture is effective only if it is maintained through the setter's delivery of the ball.

Blocking Footwork

Successful blocking starts with efficient footwork. No matter how high players jump, no matter how aggressively players reach to block the ball, they can become good blockers only through patiently learning to use footwork patterns that take them efficiently to the point of attack. The difference between getting to the ball and executing a successful block and arriving too late is often less than half a second. It is imperative that coaches select and rigorously train footwork aimed at increasing their blockers' speed and efficiency.

Outside blockers are responsible for setting the block. Against a high set, for example, they establish the outside position and become the anchor to which the middle blocker closes in the attempt to form a double block. Occasionally, when the opponent sets the ball directly in front of his or her base position, the outside blocker does not have to move in order to set the block. Usually, however, outside blockers have to adjust laterally, one direction or the other, in order to find the correct set-up position.

Right-Side Blockers

Right-side blockers can use one of two footwork patterns—the shuffle or the crossover step. If the distance between base position and set-up position is approximately 4 feet or less, the shuffle step is preferred. The leading foot is picked up first and steps in the direction the blocker intends to move. The trailing foot is the "push" foot and closes next to the leading foot to finish the move. When executing the shuffle step, the shoulders remain parallel to the net, and the blocker remains squared to the attacker from beginning to end of the move. The only drawback is that if the move is executed too slowly, the outside blocker's trailing foot—in this case, the right-side blocker's left foot—remains on the floor to push off into the shuffle and can get in the way of the middle blocker's attempt to close the block. So, if you coach your outside blockers to use the shuffle step, teach them to execute it early and with sufficient speed.

When a blocker must move more than 4 feet, the crossover step should be employed. When moving to the right, the right-side blocker's inside (left) foot lifts and crosses over in front of the outside (right) foot. The push comes from the outside (right) foot as the blocker's hips turn in the direction of the move. The upper body and hands remain square to the net. The inside (left) foot plants first; then the outside (right) foot produces the final braking action, which completes the set-up. The feet and hips have turned back to a squared position as the plant is executed. This is a more explosive move than the shuffle step and has the advantage of clearing the inside foot out of the path of the closing middle blocker.

Left-Side Blockers

Left-side blockers' options are essentially the same but have one important difference. When the opponent passes the ball to the orthodox setter position, the distance between the setter and the opponent's right-side (Area 2) attack zones is much shorter than the distance to the left-side (Area 4) attack zones. And in today's offensive schemes, the sets to Area 2 are lower and faster. This gives the left-side blocker—and the middle blocker—much less time to react than do sets to Area 4. Remember that most defensive, base position configurations place the left-side and middle blockers close together in an attempt to thwart the quick attack in the seam between Area 3 and 2. The blockers movement patterns must be perfectly choreographed so they can move efficiently and quickly as a tandem to the point of attack. The shuffle step option must be used *only* when adjusting to the left a distance of 18 to 24 inches. Otherwise, the middle blocker will step on the left-side blocker's inside (right) foot when moving to block against a set near the antenna in Area 2. This is why, in most cases, the left-side blocker should employ the crossover step when moving left to set the block.

Middle Blockers

Middle blockers have, in my opinion, the toughest assignment in the game of volleyball. They are responsible for protecting against all quick attacks in the middle zones of the net, yet are also expected to close and form tight blocks against all outside attacks. Meanwhile, opposing setters are devising ways (faking to quick hitters, disguising their delivery styles, and using head and shoulder fakes of their own) to entice the middle blocker into making a mistake. Middle blockers must be tireless, explosive jumpers with exceptional lateral speed. They are the cornerstone of any successful defense.

The most difficult assignment for any middle blocker is to guard against the quick attack and still be able to move to the outside in time to form a tight, double block. It is essential that middle blockers possess efficient, technical footwork skills. I am not going to diagram all of the various footwork patterns I have observed over the years. I believe that a coach should experiment with his or her own middle blockers, using different footwork patterns and a stop watch, to learn which patterns work best for those players. But there are a few suggestions I can offer.

First, I suggest training your middle blockers to move to the outside using the orthodox step-crossover-step move. This is by far the most widely used footwork pattern. The middle blocker waits in coiled posture to read the set direction. If the set goes to the opponent's Area 4, the middle blocker steps with the right foot, turning the hips in the direction of the move. The left foot crosses in front of the right in a running motion and becomes the initial plant foot as the blocker arrives at the outside set-up position. The right foot and hips swing into a squared position as the plant is completed. This move closely resembles a three-step spike approach, except that the upper body and hands remain square to the net throughout. The footwork patterns are reversed when closing to the left to block an attack from Area 2.

If you find that your middle blockers cannot get all the way to the outside blocker using this footwork—and this is a common problem at the lower levels of play—I recommend that you add a shuffle step prior to the first step or add a hop (off the left foot, if closing to the right; off the right foot, if closing left) before the final plant. These additional moves will allow the blocker to cover a greater distance. But you will have to live with the increased time expended in making the move.

Regardless of the footwork pattern you select, it is imperative that you train a middle blocker to position the outside foot 4 to 6 inches from the outside blocker's inside foot when planting to jump. This enables the blockers to form a tight block. If the middle blocker stops too far short of the outside blocker, there is always the danger that a seam will be left between them.

When the middle blocker cannot execute this ideal close to within 4 to 6 inches, it is better that he or she stop and jump to block at an inside position, rather than risk arriving too late at the point of attack. When this occurs, the middle blocker must decide whether to reach into the seam in an attempt to close to the outside blocker's hands, or to reach straight up and over, leaving a hole that can be read by the floor defender behind the block.

Hand Position

Hand position is critical to successful blocking. I have used the following key phrases to describe proper hand position.

Seal the Net

As the blocker pushes the hands up and over the net to block the ball, the hands must travel in an upward path in front of the blocker's body to the anticipated point of contact with the ball, while remaining within 2 to 4 inches of the net surface. This eliminates the common error of reaching backward or even straight up, thereby leaving the hands momentarily as much as 18 inches away from the net, and batting the hands toward the ball. This failure to seal the net often leads to balls being hit for points or side-outs into the space between the net and the blocker's hands.

Penetrate

This is the battle cry of the volleyball coach when teaching blocking. It seems to be such a simple concept, yet it is the most abused of all the blocking skills. The laws of geometry tell us that when attempting to tighten the attack angles, it is important to penetrate with the hands as far as possible into the opponent's court. The height of the blocker's reach is much less important, unless attempting to block an attacker who contacts the ball unusually high above the net. Reaching over is better than reaching high. Sealing and penetrating thus become complementary concepts.

Thrust

For maximum blocking efficiency, it is important that the blocking platform, which includes the hands, arms, and shoulders, is aligned in its strongest position on impact with the ball. A weak platform can result in the hands being knocked out of position, causing unpredictable and difficult-to-defend ricochets. I like blockers to say the word *thrust* to themselves as the hitter contacts the ball. This is the signal to thrust their shoulders and hands upward and forward, locking the skeletal and muscular structure of the blocking platform into place at the very moment it contacts the ball. The feeling of the thrust can be simulated if you imagine that a string is tied to each of your thumbs. The other end of each string is held by your coach, seated in the balcony above the opponent's baseline. Just as you say the word *thrust*, the coach pulls on both strings, stretching and elongating your blocking platform. Without the strings, however, the blocker must supply the movement from the shoulders, hence the term *thrust*.

One note of clarification should be added here. The thrust concept is different from the popular shoulder press technique. The press is a forward, swinging move, originating from the shoulders, aimed at batting the ball down into the opponent's court. The thrust is a stretching, locking move intended to achieve a strong and stable blocking platform.

Draw Out the Block

The success of a block can sometimes be measured in fractions of a second. The hand position must be perfect at the exact moment the ball strikes the block. The longer a blocker can maintain good hand position, the greater the chance that a successful block can be executed. Drawing out the block means that the hands should be the first part of the block to get into proper position and the last part to leave proper position. Inexperienced blockers tend to jab their hands at the ball, bringing them down quickly as they descend from their jump. Good blockers learn to keep their hands up and in good position even though their center of gravity has begun to descend. By learning this technique, blockers can compensate for minor errors in the timing of their jump. It also limits the success of the attacker's timing options (swinging early to beat the block or swinging on the way down to catch a blocker descending).

PRINCIPLES OF FLOOR DEFENSE

When I began my coaching career the only thing I knew about defensive technique was what I had learned as a beach player who sometimes played the six-man, indoor game. To me, defense was instinctive and uncomplicated. Unfettered by technical constraints about what to do and what not to do, I encouraged any reasonable attempt to keep the ball in play. Basically, I accepted whatever defensive styles players brought to the gym and then tried to blend the varying styles together into one defensive effort. Effort was important, not technique.

I will always believe that superior effort is mandatory in playing good defense. Even marginally equipped players, technically speaking, can become good defensive players if they defend with tenacity and fighting spirit. Nevertheless, I soon realized that good team defense can be enhanced by building a solid technical base.

My early efforts to incorporate defensive technical training into my practice sessions were rather mindless. Like many others in the 1970s, I became infatuated with the acrobatic techniques introduced by the Japanese national teams. I taught my players how to execute the Japanese roll. I also taught the dive. Rolling and diving became the focus of all my defensive drills. Like many other coaches of that period, I derived great satisfaction from this experience. We could now say proudly that our sport did indeed have a specific defensive, technical structure. In gyms across the country, rolling and diving dominated the defensive portion of our practice sessions. The problem was, and I think I speak for most of us, I adopted these techniques too quickly and without a critical mindset.

Through the years, I changed with the tide. When the sprawl became popular, I taught the sprawl. When diving began to disappear from women's volleyball, I stopped teaching the dive. When it became ''mandatory'' to dig with two arms instead of one before pushing into the roll, I followed suit. I agree that many of these developments were clearly good for volleyball. My point is, however, that for years, I accepted them, incorporating them into my training regimen with little critical evaluation of their worth or appropriateness.

My growing skepticism toward volleyball's conventional wisdom began to spill over into defense. I wasn't happy with the way in which I had built my philosophical foundation for teaching the defensive phase of the game. I had been keeping up with every innovation, but there was no sequential structure, no thoroughly worked out set of reasons for my approach to coaching defense. Furthermore, and this cannot be overemphasized as a factor in my decision to reevaluate my approach, I slowly began to realize that the emergency techniques (rolling, diving, and sprawling) that dominated my defensive practice time were necessary only occasionally during competition. It occurred to me that I was spending an inordinate amount of time training players in skills that would be drawn upon infrequently, at best.

By 1983, I had decided to take matters into my own hands, to forge a set of principles upon which I could build a defensive training philosophy. My first act was to take a close look at the top level of women's collegiate play to determine just what defensive skills would have to be acquired before my team could begin winning. Don Hardin and I went to the 1983 NCAA National Championships in Lexington, Kentucky, to record what we saw. We evaluated every defensive opportunity of each team in a systematic fashion. We recorded a simple hash mark for each time any of these defensive plays were made:

- Digging in place; no step required
- One step and dig; player remains on her feet
- One step and extend or collapse; player is forced to make a low move with platform pushed under and through the ball; player is forced to extend forward or laterally with forearms contacting the floor (this category included what many coaches call a *sprawl*)
- Run-through; player uses multiple running steps to track down lower velocity balls
- Dives
- Rolls
- Miscellaneous emergency moves (instinctive, quick-reaction saves)

After carefully watching four matches (two semifinal matches, a consolation, and a final) involving the best teams in the nation and recording every defensive play in each match, we came up with the following results:

- Digging in place (35%)
- One step and dig (22%)
- Extend or collapse (15%)
- Run-through (17%)
- Dive (0%)
- Roll (6%)
- Miscellaneous (5%)

Subsequent evaluation of other top level collegiate matches, as well as videotape analysis of international women's matches, such as China versus Japan and USA versus USSR, confirmed that this distribution is relatively reliable. And though there are other factors to consider in building a theoretical basis for teaching defense, some of which I will discuss later, I drew some very important conclusions from this experience.

First, I had been spending too much practice time teaching rolling, diving, and other miscellaneous, emergency moves that were being employed only a small percentage (10 to 15%) of the time in competition. I needed to begin emphasizing the fundamentals of digging in place, one-step-and-dig, and run-throughs. In other words, I needed to begin teaching my players how to control the ball while remaining on their feet. After all, these types of defensive plays were occurring, according to my research, 84% of the time!

Finally, I realized that the emergency floor move that should receive the most attention in training should be the extension, or collapse move (15%). In my opinion, rolling is merely one way to recover from a well-executed extension move. So, in my scheme of things, the extension to the ball became the focus of my emergency move training. The recovery move, whichever one seemed to work best for each player, became secondary.

With these newfound principles, I began to hammer out what was to become my foundation for teaching defense.

Balance Training

In the course of the 1986 season, I had occasion to ask Pang WuQiang to critique American collegiate women's volleyball. In a very diplomatic way, he expressed his surprise that so many players were unbalanced as they prepared to read an attack and execute a defensive maneuver. As he put it, players were "charging" on defense.

Pang was right. His observation helped to affirm in my mind something that had been bothering me for some time. My players had been unable to make certain defensive plays because of improper body position at the moment of contact by the attacker. Some were airborne, having lunged forward using a previously-learned pre-hop technique. Others were unbalanced as a result of sloppy preparation mechanics. The net result was that we were limiting the number of balls we could dig. All the platform, extension, and roll training in the world would be ineffective without first teaching the players to maintain a balanced position while reading the play. Balance training is now the first item on my list for teaching defense, and I devote a considerable percentage of training time to teaching its fundamentals.

Principles of Balance Training

I learned the intricacies of balance training from watching Jay Potter, who succeeded Don Hardin as my assistant coach, train my team. The concept is simple: At the moment the hitter contacts the ball, realizing that it is impossible to predict the direction or velocity of the shot or whether it will deflect off the block, the floor defender must be stopped and in a balanced position ready to move in any direction. Any unnecessary movement at this moment predisposes the body to move in one particular direction, and if that direction is away from the ball, the defender is going to be caught out of position. The only exception to the "stopped and balanced" rule is that when floor defenders read the tip, they are free to move into the anticipated tip area. But, as we coaches are fond of saying, they'd better be right.

To be balanced, a floor defender must stand with feet shoulder-width apart (or slightly wider), toes pointing slightly inward. If the defender has forward responsibilities in the defensive scheme, the feet must be in a stride position, one foot slightly ahead of the other. If a defender has primarily lateral responsibilities (this is often the case for the middleback player), then the feet should be in a more even, horizontal position. The weight should be forward on the balls of the feet. The defender bends at the knees and at the waist so that the knees are in front of the toes and the shoulders are in front of the knees. The elbows hang directly under the shoulders and are bent at a 90-degree angle so that the forearms are low and parallel to the floor. The head is up, and the eyes are trained on the setter-attacker-blocker configuration.

Advantages of Balance Training

Balance training eliminates several defensive mistakes, including the following:

Feet Off the Floor at Contact by the Attacker

Many athletes are taught a pre-hop move, which is executed just before contact. This move is similar in concept to the pre-hop used by tennis players preparing to receive serve. Many volleyball players, however, mistime the move and end up airborne at contact. Other players have the habit of hopping into the air to widen their stance. This is usually the result of a player never having learned to start with a wide enough base in the first place. Whatever the cause, players who are off the floor at contact have little or no chance of responding to a ball that is not hit right at them.

Raising Up at Contact

I call this the "Ed Norton" move, and it is extremely common among players at all levels. Fans of the TV show, "The Honeymooners," will recall that Ed Norton (played by Art Carney) frequently demonstrated his appreciation of a humorous event by leaning backward and waving his arms in a circular motion at his sides while uttering, "Whoooaaaa . . . va . . . va . . . voom." This is exactly what I see many defenders do at the moment of contact. Instead of making a precise, efficient move toward the ball, they raise up and backward, arms out at their sides, before moving in the direction of the ball. This unnecessary posturing severely cuts into the reaction time of the defender attempting to dig the ball.

Leaning With the Upper Body Before Contact

Many athletes tend to follow the opponent's ball circulation by leaning the upper body in response to each movement of the setter or hitters. This constant shifting of weight is dangerous, because it keeps the defender in a continuously unbalanced position. If the ball is attacked in a direction other than that of any one of these numerous weight shifts, then the defender is out of position to dig the ball.

Stepping in the Opposite Direction

Another common error in reacting to the moment of contact is to step left to go right, right to go left, forward to go backward, or backward to go forward. Usually this occurs because the defender has not attained the proper balance prior to contact and must reach in the opposite direction with one foot to get the leverage needed to push off toward the ball. This extra step not only takes the defender further away from the play, it also eats up precious reaction time.

Summarizing Balance Training

Balance training is to floor defense what coiled posture is to block training. The floor defender must be in the posture that best allows for any possible movement pattern. This can only be achieved when the defender is stopped and balanced, poised to move in any direction to make the defensive play.

Movement Training

There is a lot of information to process as a player waits in the read position, ready to defend against the opponents attack. The task is made easier when the defender makes a perfect read and is in a position to dig the ball without having to move. Usually, however, defenders must move to the ball from their read positions. To do this efficiently, defenders must accurately track a sphere moving at up to 100 mph (at the highest levels of play) and, after determining whether it is in- or out-of-bounds, decide where and how to intercept its flight. They must move their centers of gravity (including feet, legs, torso, arms, and hands) toward the ball and do so in a fashion that maximizes efficiency of movement. And while all of this is going on, they must work to position the digging platform (i.e., the configuration of shoulders, arms, and hands) so precisely that the ball will rebound toward a target near the net, where the setter is waiting.

Rules to Guide Movement Training

To defend successfully requires efficiency of movement. The available reaction time is too brief for anything less. Here are some general rules to guide the training of efficient defensive movement.

Hands to Ball First

When defending against high velocity balls, the player's first response must be to move the hands (i.e., the platform) to the ball. Any other movement would only delay the platform move, possibly causing the hands to arrive too late to dig the ball. But though this may seem an obvious axiom of defensive execution, it is violated constantly by players at all levels. The most common fault is to lift a foot and step first toward the ball, allowing the platform to trail. Another is to raise up with the body or platform (or both) in a preparatory or "cocking" action before moving the platform to the ball. And still another is to pull the platform back toward the body before shooting the hands toward the ball. All of these errors have in common the fact that they delay the efficient and immediate movement of the platform to the ball.

Developing Platform Awareness

Platform awareness is the sense a player develops of how to position the platform (given all the varied and sometimes unorthodox body positions a defender has to assume when executing a dig) so that the ball will be directed toward the setter. There are no clear rules that apply to every situation, because defenders often must free-lance and be creative when reacting to the ball. However, there are certain generalizations that can be emphasized.

First, defenders should strive to keep the platform out in front of the body, in order to maintain maximum leverage and control. Pulling the platform into the body tends to force the defender's center of gravity back onto the heels. The shoulders and chest should be hollowed or rounded, and the platform should remain firm yet not stiff. Defenders should practice deciding when to use the platform to cushion and when to drive the ball toward the setter, depending on the velocity and angle of the attack. When the ball must be directed left or right of the defender's body line, the platform angle should be altered by tilting the shoulders, thereby maintaining platform integrity. Players should avoid rolling the forearms and elbows in an attempt to redirect the ball. And finally, players must be trained to apply the proper touch with the forearms. Balls should lift softly from the platform to the setter in order to initiate a successful counterattack. Balls that pop up or shoot wildly off the forearms are more difficult for the setter to control.

Running Through to Retrieve Low Velocity Balls

The run-through move has been with us now for several years and has lodged itself firmly in defensive training manuals. When a player must move from a balanced, read position to retrieve a low velocity ball (two common examples are tips and balls deflected high off the block), he or she should turn and run to the point of interception, tilt the platform toward the setter, contact the ball on the move, and continue running through the point of contact without changing course (see Figure 4.1). The defender does not attempt to stop at the ball and swivel the hips

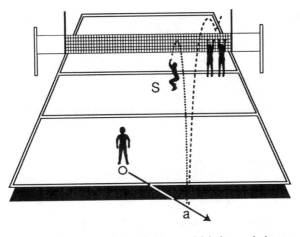

------- = Path of ball deflected high and deep
off the block
O = Starting point for defender
S = Target (setter) for defensive pass
a = Point where defender intercepts ball
·············· = Path of ball after it has been
contacted using the run-through
technique

Figure 4.1 Running through the ball.

and shoulders in an attempt to use the platform to sweep the ball to the setter. Stopping tends to cause the ball to fly off the platform with too much "juice" and too little control. The straight-through, cutting motion of the platform used in the run-through technique seems to soften the pass and increase control by imparting backspin to the ball.

There is an exception to this rule. When the ball is travelling at such a low velocity that there is ample time for the defender to move to the ball and establish a stopped, balanced position before passing the ball, the run-through move is unnecessary. Many free balls can be played in this fashion. The choice between playing the ball from a stationary position and executing a run-through is different for each player, depending on quickness and skill level.

Footwork, Extension, and Recovery Moves

Higher velocity attacks (e.g., hard spikes), which cannot be dug from a stationary, balanced position, require specific footwork, extension, and recovery patterns. The push step—some call it the jab step—is the most common footwork pattern used by defenders. The foot opposite the direction required by the defensive move becomes the push foot. For example, if a defender must move to the right to dig a ball, the left foot becomes the push foot. The right foot simultaneously lifts and steps in the direction of the ball. The push step is used to move to balls in front of and to either side of the defender.

The other footwork pattern is the crossover step and is used almost exclusively to play balls hit to either side of the defender. In this case, the foot nearest the ball becomes the push foot, and the foot opposite the ball lifts, crosses over, and steps toward the ball. This foot is then used to execute a second push that drives the defender toward the ball. The crossover step allows the digger to cover more ground than the push step will allow when digging balls hit wide to the defender's side.

The extension move is basic to all styles of going to the floor to dig hard spikes. Whether you teach the sprawl, the roll, or whatever, the principles of extending the body and platform under and through the ball still apply. As the digger steps to the ball, the hips and shoulders begin to lower in unison toward the floor. The push comes from the feet and legs. The platform drives under and through the ball. The underside of the platform (i.e., elbows and forearms) contacts the floor first. The shoulders and hips remain square to the line of flight of the attack as the platform pushes through the point of contact.

The recovery occurs only after the ball has been dug. I have no particular preference as to which of the available recovery moves is the best. I think there is some merit in assuming that, for example, anatomical differences between players predispose one player to use the barrel roll, though another might fare better with a straight-ahead, chest slide. I do not wish to belittle this area of defensive training, particularly because each player must be taught to go to the floor with abandon and not worry about being injured. I do work with my players to develop effective recovery moves, but I consider balance training and proper movement to the ball much more critical in teaching good defense. It is in these areas that I concentrate the majority of my efforts.

There is one final matter to address in discussing floor extension training. Most players make the mistake of allowing one or both knees to hit the floor before the platform contacts the ball. This derives, I think, from fear of being injured when hitting the floor. By dropping the knees first, the player is able to ease down to the floor. But though this may seem less risky to the defender, the extra motion, lowering the body to the floor from the knees, not only slows the platform extension to the ball, it also cuts down on the leverage available to the defender for digging the ball.

Situational Training

In addition to the technical implications outlined previously, there often arise in the defensive phase of the game a variety of specific situations that require attention as well.

Loose Ball

No matter how comprehensive your defensive training plan, it is impossible to incorporate and prepare for every conceivable defensive situation. Players must be ready to make instinctive, split-second moves to save a ball. These moves may not resemble anything close to the technique described previously. It might be necessary to throw a fist in the air to punch a ball straight up, or in another instance, a player may have to use an elbow to keep a sharp ricochet alive. These are called *loose balls,* and it is advisable to occasionally run drills that sharpen players' reactions to these situations.

Get-Point

Defenders must be able to determine the proper *get-point* for each ball. The get-point is the point at which the platform (or hands) intercepts the flight of the ball. This is the same skill outfielders in baseball or softball must learn in order to catch a fly ball, a wide receiver to catch a pass, or a tennis player to execute a return. To those who have nurtured this skill as youngsters, it seems natural to go automatically to the proper get-point to dig a ball. But for many, it is not natural and must be learned. These athletes tend to pursue and reach for the ball at each point along the arc of the ball's trajectory, instead of judging the point where the ball will fall, and then attempting to move quickly to the lowest possible get-point. By allowing themselves to be drawn magnetically toward the ball all the way through its flight pattern, these defenders inevitably arrive late to the get-point and are unable to make the play. Coaches should design drills that emphasize the calculation and movement mechanics that will enable players to arrive at the proper get-point.

Seam Digging

Many attacks are directed toward the seam between two floor defenders (see Figure 4.2). In this case, Player 4 and Player 5 must coordinate their

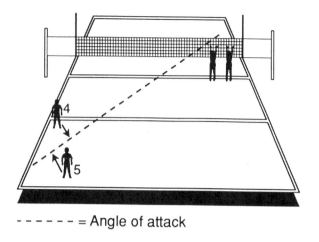

- - - - - - = Angle of attack

Figure 4.2 Seam digging.

movement patterns so they do not collide with one another while attempting to dig the ball. A widely accepted rule of thumb—one which I accept also—dictates that the two players must execute a scissor-type crossing move to cover the seam. The player closer to the point of attack (Player 4) crosses in front, and the player further from the point of attack (Player 5) crosses behind. This system provides maximum seam coverage and eliminates the possibility of a collision. Training time for seam digging must be included in the overall defensive training scheme.

Balancing the Court

Frequently during the flow of play, players find themselves out of position and unable to assume their assigned places. Perhaps a floor defender has run off the court to retrieve a ball and cannot return in time to be in base position as the opponent prepares to counterattack. Or a middle hitter has run a slide set on the right side; the ball is dug quickly, and the opponent sets to Area 2, but the slide hitter's left-to-right momentum prevents him or her from recovering in time to set a block against the attack. In these and similar instances, it is important that the team work as a unit to balance the court, to even out the spacing between the remaining players, so that no area of the court is left unprotected. As soon as the errant player is able to return, everyone can resume their normal system positions.

On-Help Position

Using a concept I borrowed from Bill Neville, former USA Men's National Team coach, I recommend special attention be given to training defenders away from the ball to assume an *on-help* position. This means that once a defender knows that he or she is not going to be involved in the first defensive contact, the defender should assume a coiled, balanced position facing the player who is making the first contact and ready to make an emergency move to play the second contact. One of my pet peeves is seeing players away from the ball relax and lose their coil, thereby rendering themselves useless if an emergency second contact is required.

Practical Issues in Training Floor Defense

As a coach prepares the seasonal plan for teaching defense, the following questions arise, and it is important that each of them be examined and resolved.

Emergency Skill Emphasis

You must decide how much emphasis (measured in units of training time) you wish to place on teaching emergency recovery moves. I put this issue before you for this reason: I see players at all levels of competition executing emergency extension and rolling techniques in attempts to make defensive plays. But I know that if they had been taught to be balanced, disciplined, and efficient in their movement skills, most—yes, I said most—of these plays could have been made without having to resort to an emergency extension or roll.

I am not calling for the elimination of extension and roll training. I am advocating that you assess the fundamental balance and movement abilities of your players, and if you find, as most of us do, that your players are deficient, that you spend most of your defensive practice time teaching the principles of balance and efficient movement. Emergency skill training can be wedged into your defensive training regimen in the early phases. But it should occupy no more than 5 to 10% of your defensive practice time, until your athletes have mastered the principles of balance and movement efficiency. Only then should you begin to build on these principles by spending more time teaching the skills that give the defensive player greater range and control in emergency situations.

Coach-Centered Versus Gamelike Drills

The debate continues to rage over whether good defense results from coach-centered or from gamelike, player-centered, defensive drill work. On one hand, the world's best defensive teams (e.g., Korea, Japan, and China) train under a coach-centered format. The coach, often standing on the floor on the same side of the net as the defenders, hits the ball at the defenders, controlling the location, speed, and degree of difficulty of each shot. The coach controls how far to push a player, when to attack the open areas of the defense, and when to hit more defensible shots that ensure a higher level of success. Under this system of training, the coach carefully monitors the rate of progress and the confidence level of each player, ultimately molding the team into a precision defensive unit.

On the other hand, current research tells us that competition-related motor skills are learned best when they are practiced exactly as they occur in competition. In other words, if, in a match, a defender must dig a ball spiked over the net and past a block, then that situation must be simulated in practice whenever defensive skills are being taught. There is little or no transfer of skills, say the experts, from an artificial, coach-centered learning format into a game situation. All drills, therefore, should be simulations of actual, competitive situations.

I find merit in both approaches. I believe that a team gets better at playing defense when it practices team defense in competitive, game situations, such as scrimmages or other six-on-six drills. Defenders must become familiar with the visual field created by game simulations. They must feel comfortable seeing the pass, the hitters running their patterns, the movement of the blockers as they converge at the point of attack, the trajectory of the set, and the body and arm positions of the attacker as the swing is executed. None of this is highlighted in coach-centered drills.

But at the same time, I believe it is important to develop a sound, defensive technical base through frequent coach-controlled repetitions of what I call "start-up" drills. You can't simply ask a nonsetter to go into a gamelike drill and start setting. There is a skill base that first must be acquired, and this base is developed through thousands of coach-controlled repetitions. The same is true for learning to play defense. Coach-controlled defensive drills are carefully structured to provide both ample time for corrective feedback between contacts and sufficient opportunity to accomplish successive levels of expertise, all of which build the athlete's confidence. I part with the experts on this one. I believe that there is substantial transfer from the coach-centered, start-up drill into the gamelike, competitive situation.

Overload and Tempo in Conducting Drills

The overload principle is applied in many areas of athletic training. It stipulates that when an athlete in training is subjected to more stimuli and at a more frequent rate than the anticipated competitive situation will present, that athlete will find it easier to cope with the demands of competition. I find this to be true in teaching defense.

There are two ways to build overload into defensive drills. The first is to test the "heart" of defensive players by asking them to dig or run down consecutive balls until they have pushed past the fatigue point of a normal match. By experiencing success in these types of drill situations, athletes find the demands of playing defense in competition easier to manage.

Another way to overload a drill is to increase the number of contacts per unit of time, or speed up the tempo of the drill. These are usually coach-initiated drills involving rapid-fire delivery of balls to the defenders. Athletes must make one play, then immediately prepare for the next. This type of overloading forces defenders not only to heighten their focus and sustain defensive intensity over a longer period of time, but also to nurture a positive disposition toward constant movement, a quality essential to playing good, team defense.

The Pursuit Rule

Coaches everywhere search for ways to motivate players during practice to go for every ball. We know that if we cannot get players to play with abandon in practice, they will not magically do so in competition. But how do we instill this competitive desire? This is a universal dilemma of coaching defense.

I used to think that getting tough and mean in defensive drills was the answer. But this yielded only temporary results. As soon as I returned to my normal, mild-mannered disposition, players stopped going for balls. I also tried reasoning with players. Going for balls can win matches, I said. Watching balls hit the floor can lead to losing. They always agreed with this extraordinary piece of logic, but balls still hit the floor. I challenged their desire to win, hoping to embarrass them into going for balls. This only chipped away at their self-esteem.

Still, I grew extremely weary of watching players make decisions about which balls they would try to dig or run down and which balls they deemed too difficult to play. I wanted to ask them just how far away the ball would have to be before they would rule it "undiggable." Eight feet, 10, 12 . . . how far? Obtaining an answer to this question would not have resulted in my team's playing better defense. But knowing just what to expect, or not expect, from my players would have reduced my stress level on the bench.

Finally, in 1984, it occurred to me that making decisions was the root of the problem. Defense is an instinctive, flow-of-play kind of skill. There is no time for rational evaluation of each defensive opportunity. The defenders must go to the ball every time. Choosing which balls to play and which not to play—this had to go.

I quickly came up with what I now call the pursuit rule and announced to my team that this rule would henceforth be a defensive commandment. The pursuit rule states that every player must do everything possible to retrieve every ball in every defensive situation. It does not matter that the ball appears to be undiggable or unretrievable. It is the unrelenting attitude of pursuit that makes a good defensive player. Going to the ball must become an instinct, a habit—not the result of rational deliberating. The pursuit rule applies universally, except for the situations listed in the following box, and these are the *only* circumstances under which the rule may be waived.

The Pursuit Rule

A player may stop pursuing the ball only if

- The ball strikes the floor or an out-of-bounds object, such as the standard, antenna, wall, or ceiling;
- Continued pursuit of the ball would risk injury;
- The referee's whistle stops play;
- A teammate clearly calls, "mine!"

In all other situations, players are expected to make their absolute best effort to save the ball. The pursuit rule has gone a long way toward solving the problem of motivating players to go to the ball. It is simple, concise, and leaves little room for interpretation.

Wrap-Up

A multitude of ideas compete for your attention when you decide on a plan for building a defensive system. As coach, you need to investigate each of the competing alternatives: Which blocking system should be deployed? How should back row defenders be arranged in relation to the block? I have my answers to these questions and you will have yours. One dictum, however, supersedes all other considerations. Once you settle on a defensive philosophy, stick to it! *What* you teach is not as important how *consistently* you teach it. Be sure that your expectations remain high for every practice session, and that your standards for correct technical execution are the same for each drill. Plan your system, and then apply an unswerving commitment to teach it. The latter, more than the former, will result in your team's playing good defense.

University of Illinois Volleyball:

A Photo Album

THE FUNDAMENTALS
OFFENSE

PASSING

SPIKING

SETTING

DEFENSE

BLOCKING

GING

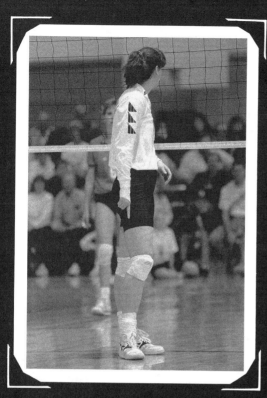

THE PRIMARY
HITTER SIGNALS
A "1" TO THE
SETTER

ILLINOIS DEPLOYS A FOUR-PERSON RECEPTI
PATTERN DURING A 1990 MATCH AGAINST
BIG 10 FOE WISCONSIN

COACH MIKE HEBERT

NT COACH DON HARDIN CONFERS
COACH HEBERT

LAURA BUSH RECEIVES INSTRUCTIONS FROM
COACH HEBERT DURING THE 1987 NCAA
CHAMPIONSHIPS IN INDIANAPOLIS

SETTER
DISA JOHNSON

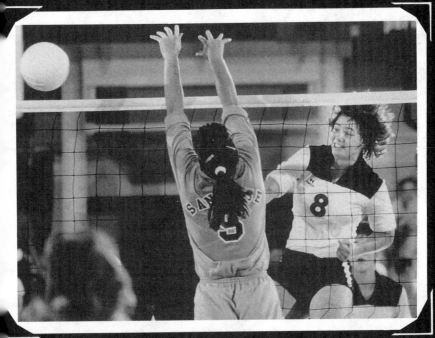

"BORN WINNER" MARY EGGERS

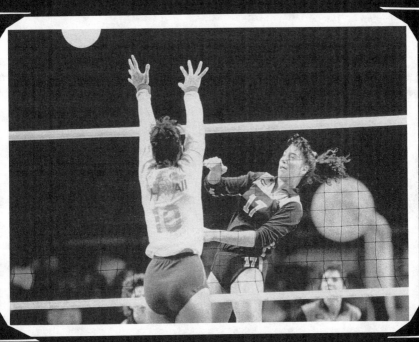

NANCY BROOKHART HITS OFF THE TOP OF
THE HAWAII BLOCK IN THE 1988 NCAA
SEMIFINAL MATCH

THE UNIVERSITY OF ILLINOIS VOLLEYBALL
TEAM CELEBRATES THE 1988 BIG 10
CHAMPIONSHIPS

Setting Goals:
The Road to Success

In February 1988, 8 weeks after participating in our first Final Four, Don Hardin and I were driving with our wives to Colorado for a few days of skiing. We were half-way through the long, flat, Kansas stretch, and it was three o'clock in the morning. We began talking about the season and our impressions about why things had gone so well, so according to plan. After winding our way through several interesting and relevant topics, I finally asked Don, if you had to limit your response to one sentence, what would you point to as the central reason for our success at Illinois? His response was very instructive. "The absolute bottom line on why our teams have won," he said, "is that we came in there and sat down and *declared* that it was going to happen."

THE PURSUIT OF GOALS

I would agree. The fact that we set out from the very beginning in 1983 with an unswerving belief in and commitment to the idea that Illinois would become an elite program is at the heart of any explanation for the team's eventual success. And as I look back through my career I can see that this very phenomenon—the establishment and pursuit of specific goals—has been the cornerstone in the foundation of my success as a coach.

Goals at Pitt

When I took the coaching job at Pitt in 1976, I was a novice as a program builder. I had never planned a budget, designed a practice, or held a team meeting. I had never seen my team play, nor had I seen any of our opponents play. In fact, I had never seen a women's volleyball match before taking the job. I gathered the players together in August and started asking a few questions. Who do we play? Who do you think we can beat? Where did we finish last season? And finally, Where do you think we can finish this season? Pitt had finished 12th in the region in 1975 and had lost some key players. "But we think we can repeat our 12th-place finish." This was their answer. And for reasons I cannot explain I responded by saying, "Why 12th—why not 4th?" The players looked uncomfortably around the room at each other. But they chose not to mount any open resistance against their new coach. And so it came to pass that the Pitt volleyball team in 1976 declared as its team goal that it would finish 4th in the Eastern AIAW Championships.

And that is exactly where we finished. We were seeded eighth heading into the regional championships and had to play the number one seed in the quarterfinal round. To everyone's surprise, including mine, we won an easy 3-0 match. We advanced to the semifinals, where we were beaten 3-1, and then lost 3-1 again in the play-off for third place. But we had finished fourth, right where we said we would.

 I started to think that I had discovered a trade secret. All you had to do was name your finish ahead of time and, presto, that's where you would finish. I called another team meeting before the 1977 season and asked the same questions. Together we reasoned that even though we had lost some key players to graduation and our schedule had been strengthened we still had enough to replicate the previous year's finish. Let's finish fourth again, we said. And we did.

By the beginning of the 1978 season I was ready to be greedy. We had what looked to be our best team ever. I was growing cocky as a goal setter. I called for the traditional team meeting. But this time I told the players that I was tired of finishing fourth. I told them that we were going to flat-out win the regional championship that year. Again, apprehensive glances shot back and forth. But no one openly balked. Four months later we breezed through the Eastern AIAW Regional Championships, claiming the title without losing a game.

Our goal in 1979 was to repeat as regional champs and go back to the AIAW National Championships. We did just that and finished, as we had in 1978, in a tie for ninth in the nation by falling one pool win short of reaching the final eight at the nationals.

By this time I knew that I had stumbled onto something important. Each time we had set a goal before the season the team accomplished that goal. At this point I didn't fully understand the psychological mechanisms at work. But I knew first-hand that there was indeed a critical connection between goals and team performance.

Goals at New Mexico

In 1980 I left Pittsburgh to take over the volleyball program at the University of New Mexico. My new team had finished last in their conference in 1979, and I knew I had a major rebuilding task in front of me. Naturally, the first thing on my agenda was to meet with the team to decide how successful we would be. But the situation was a bit different this time. The conference schedule included some highly successful teams, such as Utah State (national champions in 1978), BYU, and Colorado State. And we were competing in what was to become the new NCAA West Region, which included teams like UCLA, Stanford, and USC. Winning a conference or regional championship was out of the question at this point. I realized that I would have to become a more creative and realistic goal setter.

We decided that we would come roaring out of last place, qualify for the postseason conference tournament (the top 6 of 11 teams qualified), and pull off one major upset over a higher seeded team at the tournament. And, of course, that's what we did. We improved to sixth, qualifying for the 1980 Intermountain Athletic Conference Tournament. In our first round we drew the University of Utah, the second seed. Again, this time to everyone's surprise *but* mine, we cruised to a relatively easy 3-1 victory. We lost in the next round to Colorado State and finished the year with a 13-20 record, but not before accomplishing our seasonal goals.

In 1981 and 1982, similar experiences were recorded. The highlights included Top Twenty rankings, all-conference player selections, and the first-ever appearance by a New Mexico volleyball team in an NCAA tournament. Now the table was set as far as I was concerned. I had honed my program-building skills at two different institutions. I had experienced great success. I felt self-assured that I had discovered the secret to winning volleyball matches. So when the offer came from the University of Illinois to coach its women's volleyball team, I knew that I was a person in the right place at the right time.

Goals at Illinois

But when I arrived in Champaign, Illinois, in August 1983, I was not prepared for what I found. I knew that I would have to recruit better players. And I knew that I would have to create a winning attitude. However, I underestimated just how far the program had slipped into disarray. Volleyball seemed to be at the bottom of *everyone's* priority list. Maintenance staff, facility schedulers, sports information personnel, athletic department administrators—all had become comfortable with the notion that volleyball was a sport that required little of their time or effort.

Our players had no locker room of their own. Our practice facility was not secure. I remember how astonished I was when, during our first practice session, the dismissal bell rang and students from nearby classrooms walked right across the floor and through our drills on their way out of the building. It was as if we didn't exist.

Things got worse. At one of our early home matches we arrived at Kenney Gym to find that there were no team benches. The maintenance crew had taken all of our folding chairs over to the football stadium to provide overflow seating for the numerous high school bands participating in Band Day at halftime. Experiences like this left an indelible impression on all of us as to just where we stood on the Fighting Illini totem pole.

Fostering Respect

I realized that the hole out of which my new program had to climb was much deeper than I had anticipated. In addition to having very little talent on the team, I was faced with having to fight organizational battles on virtually every front just to keep the program functioning on a day-to-day basis. I made a judgment call. There would be no performance goals for the 1983 season. Instead, we would work to establish the principles upon which the program would be built in the future and, in doing so, begin to reshape the perceptions that people held of our program.

This turned out to be a wise decision. We fought our way to a 5-25 record that year, good for last place in the Big Ten. "What happened?" my friends asked me. "I don't know," I answered. "I don't know how we won those five matches." But we had begun to make considerable headway in creating an atmosphere of respect both within and outside of our program. The principles of hard work, accountability, honesty, and self-respect and been locked into place among the athletes. And I had spent countless hours, both locally and throughout the region, speaking to coaches and civic groups, laying the public relations groundwork for the inevitable success I projected for the team. As we prepared for the 1984 campaign, I felt that we had taken a giant step forward on the self-esteem spectrum.

Setting Performance Goals

It was time to return to performance goal setting. We decided that we would win eight matches in the conference that year, four times as many as the year before. As it turned out we played well enough to win more than eight. But we lost all of our down-to-the-wire matches and, despite finishing over .500 (18-15) for the first time in 6 years, ended up winning only six in the conference. But along the way, I stumbled across a goal-setting device that was to become an important building block in creating the success of the Illinois program.

Early in the Big Ten season, we stood at 3-1 and had to face a very tough Purdue team that had won three of the last five conference championships and were challenging again in 1984. A year earlier, they had dealt my Illinois team the worst defeat I have ever experienced as a coach. I knew my players were intimidated, yet I knew there had to be something I could do to avoid the doom that was sure to settle in as we prepared for the match. Then it struck me. I called for a closed-door meeting with the team. No one knows this except us, I told them, but we are going to spring the biggest surprise of the season. We are going to upset Purdue on Friday night. The players were in shock. Some stared back at me with wide eyes. Some giggled. But by the time we left the meeting, everyone had bought into the hare-brained idea that lowly Illinois would pull off the shocker of the season.

Everything we did that week in practice was reinforced with talk of the upset. By Wednesday players were even smiling at one another, getting a little cocky. On Friday night we took the floor, and we were a different team—a confident, aggressive team. We didn't win the match. But we almost did. We fought Purdue tooth and nail, losing to them in four tough games (13-15, 9-15, 16-14, 14-16). But in the minds of our players, it was as good as a win. By creating in themselves the belief that they could beat Purdue, they learned firsthand about the power of thoughts in influencing performance. And I learned that there are times when a seemingly hopeless situation, a situation where all the cards seem to be stacked against you, can be transformed into a marvelous opportunity to accomplish the impossible.

Contributions of Mary Eggers

The 18-15 record was certainly an improvement over 5-25. But it didn't accurately measure the progress the team was making in terms of its self-concept. We were gradually learning how to think like winners, behave like winners. The attitude was infectious, so infectious that we began to recruit some of the country's top players. One of these players was Mary Eggers.

In 1985 Mary arrived in Champaign and had an immediate impact on the program. In its preseason goal-setting meeting, the team decided to shoot for a top three finish in the Big Ten. This would put us in position for a possible postseason NCAA tournament berth. We had fallen just short of our goals in 1984, because a few things didn't go our way. But in 1985 everything was to go our way, and one of the most important things going for Illinois was Mary Eggers, on our side of the net. She was a talented quick hitter, maybe one of the best ever. But even more important, she was a born winner. No, that's not strong enough. Mary Eggers absolutely hated to lose. She became so filled with disgust when we fell behind in a match that she single-handedly would will our team to victory. She taught our team how to win even when we weren't in the mood.

We ran off an incredible 30 victories in a row to start the season. Illinois volleyball was becoming a big deal. We began selling out Kenney Gym for home matches. Local and national media attention increased. We had become the Cinderella team of 1985.

We eventually lost another heartbreaker to Purdue (15-13 in the fifth game) to finish 16-2 to their 17-1 in the conference. But we were selected to the NCAA tournament. After upsetting Western Michigan in the first round, we lost in the regional semifinals to Chuck Erbe's USC Trojans. We ended the year with a 39-3 record. Eggers and our other middle blocker, Denise Fracaro, were named to the all-Big Ten first team. I was named national NCAA Coach of the Year. And our program had jumped several rungs on the prestige ladder, finishing the season as the nation's 10th-ranked team. But still, we kept an accurate perspective. A reporter once asked Don Hardin to explain the successes of the 1985 season. "That's easy," he said. "We recruited Mary Eggers."

I agree with him. Yes, all the building blocks had been carefully laid in place. But in 1985, I learned yet another lesson in goal setting and program building: To vault from the pack, to distinguish yourself from the others who are also dedicated to achieving high level success, you need a little luck. We would have been good in 1985 without Mary, but we never would have accomplished what we did. Her performances, her impact on the team's mentality allowed us to skip several developmental stages on our journey to the top. We knew she would be good when we recruited her. But we didn't know she was *that* good. That part of it was luck.

In 1986 Don Hardin and I sat down to hammer out our seasonal goals. We were now in a new ball game. Playing the part of the underdog and pulling off the surprise season was an easy task compared to having to follow it up with another solid, elite-level effort. You know the old saying, Getting there is easy, staying there is tough. But we had an experienced setter in junior Disa Johnson; Eggers was returning for her sophomore year; and we had recruited another tremendous middle-blocking prospect in Nancy Brookhart. It was time to go for it. We decided to shoot for winning the Big Ten and then to advance all the way to the finals of the NCAA Regional Championships, taking the program one step further than the previous year on both counts.

The Power of Words

I was about to get my next lesson in goal setting. As I struggled with how to convince our players that they were probably good enough to win the conference championship, Don's mind was on a different course. I was concerned that in 1985 we had skipped too many rungs in the ladder and that asking for an improvement on that performance might be too great a burden for our young team. But Don had the answer. We're not simply going to win the Big Ten, he reasoned, we're going to *clinch* the title at home against our archrival Purdue (with two regular season matches remaining). This was brilliant. By the use of one word *clinch*, he wiped out any possibility of doubt in the minds of the players. This was a bold, aggressive statement. It turned a "maybe we can win it" attitude into a "we're going to win it going away" certitude. And while we were at it, we were going to do it against the dreaded Purdue Boilermakers. I'll always be indebted to Don Hardin for this shrewd piece of goal setting.

We stormed through the conference schedule that year, finishing with a perfect 18-0 record and the first-ever Big Ten championship for a women's sport at Illinois. We did, in fact, clinch the title with a victory over Purdue. We were 36-3 overall, ranked in the top ten all season, and Mary Eggers was named all-American. Everything had gone according to plan, until our two freshmen phenoms, Nancy Brookhart and Bridget Boyle, were ruled out of the NCAA tournament because of illness and injury, respectively. Now we had to play without two important starters. After winning our first-round match against Northern Iowa, we again had to go up against a very good Western Michigan team in the regional semifinals. The match turned out to be a testimony to the power of goal setting. All year we had focused on winning this match to get one step closer to reaching the coveted Final Four. I watched with amazement as our depleted lineup easily handled Western Michigan, this time in three quick games. We lost in the final to Nebraska. But once again, we accomplished exactly what we had set out to accomplish, despite the loss of key personnel.

The 1987 season began with the same dilemma: How do we stay among the nation's elite? Everyone wanted a piece of us. This is part of the territory when you win. Fending off challengers and keeping your eye fixed on the road ahead—this is the difficult task. Having established our dominance in the conference, our attention turned toward the post-season: the Final Four—this was our goal. We didn't do anything fancy with the wording of our goals. Win the Big Ten again, and then the regional championship—these things speak for themselves.

Redirecting Negative Energy

Now I was about to experience my next firsthand lesson in the art of setting and pursuing goals. We suffered an early-season loss to Nebraska, our principal rival in the mideast region. It was a long, five-game match that we had been in a position to win several times. The loss had a demoralizing effect on our team. Again, Don Hardin had the answer. Let's harness all of this negative energy and redirect it, he said. Let's dedicate our entire season, from this moment on, to achieving a victory over Nebraska when we play them again in the regional championships. We held a brief meeting in the hotel before returning to Champaign. The players enthusiastically bought into the plan. And from then on, at least once during every practice session, we talked about how we would beat Nebraska in the regionals. We prepared, modified, and refined our game plan several times. We looked at hours of videotape. We developed a healthy obsession with the fact that we would avenge our earlier loss.

As my team left the team meeting before taking the floor against Nebraska in the finals of the 1987 Mideast Regional Championships, I knew we were going to win the match. We were supremely confident. We had planned so carefully, and we had told ourselves for so long and in so many positive ways that we would win. As the match unfolded, my confidence grew. I can remember vividly, thinking as I looked at the scoreboard in Game 3 (we had won the first two games), and saw us ahead 12-5, We did it, just like we said we would.

Illinois defeated Nebraska 3-0 that night, qualifying for our first trip to the Final Four. And I learned that a coach must remain vigilant to the emotional swings of the team during the season. There may be occasions, as there were for us following our early-season loss to Nebraska, when you can capture the moment to formulate new goals or, as in our case, enhance already existing ones.

Both of our goals for the 1987 season had been realized. We won the Big Ten championship with a 17-1 record, and we won the regional championship with our win over Nebraska. Mary Eggers and Nancy Brookhart were both named all-Americans. We were 31-7 overall and finished the year ranked fifth in the nation. We lost a close match to Hawaii, the eventual champion, in the national semifinals and finished in a tie for third with Texas. In the process I learned one more lesson about team goals, and I would like to share this observation before moving on.

Setting Inclusive Goals

The lesson is this: When you are preparing to win a championship, your goal must be to do just that—win the *championship* match. And when you put all your eggs in that basket, you simply have to cross your fingers and trust that fate will deal you a fair hand as you make your way through the preliminary qualifying events. I don't think teams can operate with multiple "goal peaks." For example, you can't ask a team to set a separate goal to win a first-round play-off match, then to win a semifinal match, and then another goal to win a championship match. To be properly motivating, goals must be singular and all-inclusive. You must not have too many of them during a season. Nothing demonstrated this fact to me more clearly than agonizing through our regional semifinal match against Western Michigan that year.

We were so focused on our showdown with Nebraska that we were a notch below good in our first-round win over Pittsburgh. And when we took the floor against Western Michigan in the next round, we were clearly a team biding its time until we could be let off the leash to go after Nebraska. Western Michigan, on the other hand, was a senior-dominated team that had grown weary of losing to Illinois in the NCAA play-offs. What transpired that night was one of the most hard-fought matches I've ever witnessed at any level. After almost 3 hours of battle we found ourselves down 9-5 in the fifth game. There wasn't much to say during the time-out. Believe in yourselves, was about all I could come up with.

We came back to win 15-10 and salvaged our dream. But I've thought a great deal about that match since then. Any team that has its sights on winning a championship will likely encounter some tough sledding on the way to the championship match. It can't be avoided. This is why some very good teams in all sports are beaten in upsets during the early rounds of the play-offs. Winning a championship requires an intense level of focus, so much so that it is impossible to generate that same level of focus for preliminary matches. We were fortunate against Western Michigan that night. But, like all other teams who perform well in the championship event, once we got past them, we were running full steam ahead for our encounter with Nebraska.

The question facing us before the 1988 season was how to follow up our success in 1987. We lost four seniors from that team, including our setter and captain, Disa Johnson. And our new setter, Barb Winsett, was slowly rehabilitating from off-season knee surgery. Do we try to improve on our finish and shoot for a national title? Or do we face reality and realize that merely repeating our 1987 performance would be a severe challenge? *Volleyball Monthly Magazine* didn't help matters by naming us their preseason favorite to win the national championship. We had some premier players, but I also knew we had some weaknesses. We were definitely not the best team in the country. But I felt that very few teams ever have the opportunity to contend for a national title and that I would be letting my players down if we settled on anything less than a national championship as our seasonal goal.

In our preseason team meeting in August, we settled on the following goals:

1. Win the Hawaii Tournament in September (Hawaii, UCLA, Pepperdine, and Illinois).
2. Win the Mid-American Classic (Texas, Kentucky, Long Beach State, and Illinois).
3. Clinch the Big Ten championship before our final conference road swing to Iowa and Minnesota.
4. Win the national championship.

The Role of Luck

This was to be the year that I learned about the other side of the luck coin. In 1985 we had had good luck in the recruiting of Mary Eggers. Our bad luck in 1988 was that Winsett's knee injury kept her from reaching her potential that season. Without a healthy, confident setter, you are not going to win a national championship. This was evident when we got to Hawaii. We were supposed to win the tournament. Instead, we were beaten by both UCLA and Hawaii and finished a disappointing third. We went into an emotional tailspin and for a long time did not play anything like a top-ranked team. The fact that we had lofty goals pushed our team to fight its way back to form. We eventually began playing well again, beating Long Beach State in the Mid-America finals and winning the Big Ten with a perfect 18-0 record for our third straight conference championship. In fact, we cruised to another Mideast regional championship, defeating Oklahoma in the finals, despite having our predictable semifinal scare against Notre Dame.

But when we arrived in Minneapolis for our second straight Final Four appearance, I knew we were on shaky ground. The injury to Winsett had kept us off balance all year. She couldn't maintain a regular practice regimen. There were plays in some matches—critical plays—that she just couldn't make. Her confidence and the team's efforts to sustain confidence in her were undergoing constant strain. The cumulative effect on our team was just enough to distract us in our pursuit of the championship. We faced Hawaii again in the semifinals. After losing a nightmarish 15-1 first game, we came back to play them dead even, eventually losing an extremely close 3-1 decision.

Our goal of a national championship remained unfulfilled. Our seniors, especially Eggers, were devastated. But reflecting on the experience, I think I understand what happened. In all but one of the previous years during my career, luck had been on my side as far as key injuries are concerned. I had never had to contend with this as a distraction. The one year I was faced with the problem, during the NCAA playoffs in 1986, I adjusted my goals downward. I knew we couldn't beat Nebraska in the finals without Brookhart and Boyle. And I knew we had to shift our goal focus to the semifinal match to have a chance of beating Western Michigan. This resulted in our stellar performance in the semifinals and, likewise, in our mediocre, uninspired effort in the finals. In 1988 I chose not to adjust downward. I stayed with the national title goal even though I knew the injury to Winsett had become a critical problem. I don't think I would handle it any differently today. I believe that you have to reach for the brass ring if you ever manage to get close. But the ripple effect of an injury to a key player can work its way into the emotional fabric of a team and, without your being able to do anything about it, can be just enough of a distraction that the all-encompassing focus required to achieve a goal becomes virtually impossible. Such was our fate in 1988, and I learned again that it is not enough to have skill as a goal setter. You must also have that thing called luck.

The 1989 season was to bring more of the same. We were ranked fourth in the AVCA preseason poll. I felt good about our team, despite the loss of Eggers to graduation. Winsett had recovered and was playing her best volleyball. We decided to set goals to repeat as Big Ten champs, ambush Nebraska in Lincoln in a late-season dual match, and win a third straight regional championship. This would send us to the Final Four in Honolulu.

But once again good fortune abandoned us. Our outstanding, two-time all-American middle blocker, Nancy Brookhart, had suffered a knee injury, which required surgery. Her recovery, like Winsett's the year before, was slow and painstaking. This was supposed to be Nancy's finest hour, her senior season in which she would lead us back to the Final Four. Instead, she was barely able to move around the court. Her extraordinary hitting and blocking skills were greatly reduced, and she was forced to play the season within the confines of her injury. It is a credit to her ability and maturity that she still compiled a .410 hitting efficiency and again was named to the all-American second team. Nevertheless, her injury had exactly the same effect on our team as did

Winsett's injury in 1988. Nancy was unable to practice with the team, playing only in certain matches. She could no longer do some of the fantastic things on the court that she had been able to do in earlier seasons. Nancy and her teammates did a marvelous job of fighting through their frustrations. But in the end, it was too great an obstacle to overcome.

Other bizarre problems occurred. The sun had been shining brightly on the Illinois program for some time. Now, Murphy's law was taking over. Two of our starters, Barb Winsett and Laura Bush, were involved in a violent head-to-head collision going for a ball. Both required emergency medical attention and were forced to sit out for a period of time. Bush later developed severe patellar tendonitis. Another starter missed some key matches after contracting viral encephalitis. Illnesses and injuries kept hitting us at every turn. In fact, we did not practice *once* that entire season with our starting lineup.

We managed to finish 27-8 and ended the year as the nation's seventh-ranked team. But we surrendered the Big Ten title to Ohio State, losing twice to them in long, five-game matches. We did, however, manage to salvage our goal of beating Nebraska in the "ambush" in Lincoln. We were selected as an at-large entry into the NCAA championships and worked our way back to the regional finals, including a hard-fought victory over Ohio State in the semifinals. But we were no match for Nebraska the next night. Our fuel tank had run dry. The injury to Brookhart, coupled with the accumulation of all the other illnesses, injuries, and distractions left us less than a worthy contender in the finals. As Nancy told the press after the match, "We were fighting a losing battle." And once again I was struck with the realization that no matter how skillful the goal setter, no matter how much one believes in the process of organizing a seasonal plan around those goals, a team must be blessed with the good fortune to avoid key injuries and the crippling emotional influence they can have.

CONCEPTS IN GOAL SETTING

As I scan over my first 14 seasons as a Division I coach, I must admit to the inescapable conclusion that setting challenging, yet reachable goals has played a major role in my success. I am frequently struck by the simplicity of the process. Yet I know from firsthand experience that it is also a complicated business, filled with hidden nuances and delicate moments requiring wisdom and sound judgment. Nevertheless, coaches who seek to scale new heights and condition their teams to become winners must learn the subtleties of goal setting. Without ability in this area, the coaches, like the captain who stands helplessly at the wheel of a ship without a rudder, can only hope that their programs can manage to stay on course and achieve success.

The Influence of the Unconscious Mind

I may have started out in 1976 as a novice in the art of setting goals. But the power of goals and their influence on team performance led me to investigate their inner workings. I am not at all sure how strictly I followed the principles of scientific inquiry, nor how much that matters to me, one way or the other. What I am sure about, however, is that I have been able to establish, at least for myself, a working model for understanding and explaining the psychology of the successful pursuit of goals.

The single, most important thing to accept—if you are going to buy into this discussion—is the existence of the unconscious mind. This should not be a troubling proposition for most people. Although they can't scientifically locate or verify its physical properties, the vast majority of modern psychologists accept that it exists. The unconscious mind, they say, is programmed by our thoughts and perceptions of reality. These thoughts and perceptions accumulate over a lifetime. This unconscious program then functions as a determinant influence on the conscious mind. Therefore, the content of this unconscious programming is a critical factor in shaping conscious behavior.

A second postulate is also important to an understanding of goal setting. The programming of the unconscious mind—and herein lies goal setting's fundamental secret—is subject to intentional modification. In other words, we can plan, structure, and control the input to our unconscious mind if we so desire. As a rule, most people go through life with the programming they acquired in childhood. If they are lucky, it is a program that serves them well. But many, if not most of us, are burdened with the programming that comes from the normal accumulation of childhood fears, defensiveness, negative thinking, and anxieties. And for many athletes, this childhood programming becomes an obstacle to achieving success in the competitive arena.

Winning in athletics demands that players possess a solid self-esteem and an unshakable level of confidence. But most athletes are underequipped to face this demand, having available only the obsolete, unconscious program that was fashioned during childhood. To face these new realities, athletes need a new program. How to create this new program and keep it operative as an athlete strives to compete—this is at the heart of the issue of setting goals.

Programming for Athletic Success

Taken together, the two principles provide the basis for a goal-setting model. If we can control the content of our unconscious mind, we can control our conscious behavior. And in athletics this translates into if we can program our unconscious mind to believe in certain performance goals, then the chances of realizing those goals are greatly enhanced.

A great deal of research has been directed toward discovering the best techniques for reprogramming the unconscious mind. The first step is to provide content for the program. This is usually done by formulating specific directives for guiding future behavior. For example, in athletics these directives, or goals, may take the following form:

- I will face every moment of adversity in competition with confidence and the will to win.
- I will be a source of positive feedback to myself and my teammates no matter how tempting the urge to be negative.
- I will be alert and undistracted during competition.

Or, when these directives take on a team flavor, they might read like these:

- We will clinch the Big Ten championship by defeating Purdue at home on November 16.
- We will win the regional championship and qualify for the Final Four.
- We will ambush Nebraska in Lincoln in our November 11th match.

Having articulated the content of the directives, it is now necessary to communicate them to the unconscious mind so that they become part of the operative programming. From what I have learned from both the psychological literature and practical experience, there are three fundamental ways to accomplish this. First, we formulate affirmations. Second, we develop visualizations. And third, *we act as if we had already accomplished our goal.*

Affirmations

Affirmations are statements that our goals are going to happen. Many times they are simple restatements of the actual goals. They are repeated over and over in each athlete's mind throughout the goal-pursuing experience, which helps to train the unconscious mind to believe in the projected outcomes. They serve to repress obsolete programming and replace it with the new. Let me give you an example.

While at Pitt in 1979, I sensed that my team was losing its focus as the season wound down toward the regional championships. At that time I understood very little about the theory of goals and their psychological function in a team setting. But instinctively I knew I had to do something to get my team back on track. I tried all sorts of things in practice. But I also did something quite unusual. I made every player write 1,000 times, I am not a quitter, I am a winner. I made them turn it in the next day before practice. This way I knew they each would have to write all 1,000 repetitions in one sitting, thereby ensuring that they would have the phrase deeply imprinted in their minds. This was not an extremely popular assignment among my players. It took most of them hours to complete. But we did go on to win the regional championship that year. I'm not sure that my little exercise had anything to do with our eventual success, but I'm not sure that it didn't either. In any case, I look back on this episode and realize that, as crude as it was, I had asked my players to engage in a fundamental experience in affirmation.

Since then my affirmation technique has become more sophisticated. I now ask players to write lengthy, goal-specific letters to me. In these letters they spell out what they intend to accomplish, as individuals and as a team. These letters become the kickoff experience in formulating affirmations for the upcoming season. Each player continually refines her list of affirmations as circumstances and conditions evolve. They are well thought out; they are specific to the challenges we confront as a team; and they are always immediately accessible. They are a fundamental part of Illinois volleyball.

Visualizations

Visualizations are mental pictures of affirmations. Visualizing gives color, depth, taste, smell, sound, and feel to the printed affirmation. If an athlete affirms that she wants to perform with confidence, then she has to learn to visualize, in as much detail as possible, what that looks like in her mind. She must see herself on the court in a tough situation, feel the fear associated with it, and then feel the surge of confidence as she responds. She must see the ball being attacked, hear the crowd roar, feel her body respond to the confident command to perform, and see the perfect execution of the play. This is visualizing the affirmation.

The same is true for team goals. All players must see in the mind's eye the enactment of our team's victory over Purdue to win the conference championship. I want them to conjure up as much detail as possible, so that their mental programming can be as complete as possible. I believe in the power of visualization. Before every match I lead my team through a 5- to 10-minute visualization session on the game plan to be followed that evening. It takes practice to develop good visualization skills, but learning them pays great dividends.

Acting "As If"

Finally, I teach my players to act as if they had already accomplished their goals. This seems to me to be a combination of affirming and visualizing, a fantasy-like acting out of the goal. Here is what I mean. When we plan our team travel, for example, we always make arrangements for whatever postseason competition we have affirmed that we would win. In all of our team meetings and practices, we always talk about *when* we advance to the regional finals, not *if*. We never allow any reference to the possibility that our goals might not be realized. We act as if our success were already a certainty.

I remember when I was in Cuba in 1987 with the USA Women's National Team. It was February, and when I returned to Champaign, I was scheduled to sit with my own team to formulate our goals for the upcoming season. At the airport in Havana, while waiting for the flight home, I saw a cigar stand. I am not a smoker, but there I was—confronted with the unique opportunity to buy real Cuban cigars.

Then it hit me. I'll buy two cigars, one for me and one for Don Hardin. We'll light them up in the locker room right after winning the regional championship and qualifying for our first Final Four. I bought the cigars, put them in my briefcase, and set them on my desk when I got back to the office. This was another of several cocky things I have done acting as if my goals would indeed come true.

Don and I did light the cigars in the locker room after our win over Nebraska. After one or two puffs, we were sick to our stomachs, and our players were razzing us for befouling the air. It wasn't much of a cigar-centered celebration. But those cigars had already served their purpose by staring at me all season from my desk top. I had committed myself in February to winning a regional championship and the two cigars were a daily reminder of that fact.

Programming in the Alpha State

Successful programming of the unconscious mind requires one last explanation. We can direct input to our unconscious most efficiently, say the researchers, when we achieve the alpha state. Brain waves are measured in cycles per second (cps). Eighty percent of our psychological time is spent in the beta state (14 cps or higher). In this state we are wide awake and our consciousness is dominated by rational thought, speech, organization, and computation. The alpha state (7 to 14 cps) is our most creative state. Most of us experience alpha as we fall asleep or wake up. We are only passively aware; we are relaxed. We are more intuitive, and we tend to experience our thoughts in pictures or images, rather than the more deliberate, logical patterns of thought construction that occur in beta. It is during the alpha state that we can most successfully affect the programming of our unconscious mind.

Researchers have also learned that we do not have to wait for our brains to naturally achieve the alpha state just before or after sleep. Through the use of self-directed relaxation techniques, anyone can slow down the brain's activity to the alpha stage. These techniques usually involve deep breathing and muscular tensing and relaxing, along with the use of imagery to induce a relaxed state of mind. Other techniques, such as those used in transcendental meditation, can be effective as well. It is not important how the alpha state is achieved, only that it is achieved. Once the athlete has slowed to alpha, it is time to start feeding new material to the unconscious mind, that is, to begin repeating the planned affirmations over and over and to create the accompanying visualizations in vivid detail. It is also helpful to do all of this as often as possible when in the normal beta state. But the reprogramming that we are after occurs more efficiently and more permanently when we learn proper relaxation techniques and organize the thoughts we want to instill in our unconscious mind in the alpha state.

Kinds of Goals

There is a great deal of discussion over what kinds of goals coaches and athletes should be setting in the team sport context. Should goals be individual- or team-centered? Should they be outcome- (winning vs. losing) or performance-centered (independent of winning or losing)?

Team Versus Individual Goals

I think both are important, but I believe that team goals should be the primary focus for everyone in the program. Individual goals can be established and pursued within the one-on-one coach/player relationship. But they should never distract from overall team goals. Let me illustrate.

In 1984 I had a player who was struggling with her hitting percentage. She made numerous unforced errors, her shot selection was poor, and, not surprisingly, her confidence as a hitter was spiraling downward. Together we began setting individual performance goals. Before one particular match, I told her that out of 10 sets, I wanted her to score 5 kills and commit only 2 errors. This would give her a hitting efficiency of .300, a very good percentage for an outside hitter. She went out that night and did exactly that. Afterward she explained that by quantifying her performance in that fashion she was able to concentrate on each swing and its mathematical function in achieving her goal, rather than feeling the usual sense of fear that had accompanied every attack opportunity until then. Having a specific individual goal greatly enhanced her performance.

But after several matches, I began to notice that a problem was emerging. This player became so internally motivated by her mathematical goal that she was losing touch with the emotional course of the match. Her numbers were improving, but her contribution to the team's chemistry was declining. Winning matches requires that each player remain, from start to finish, fully attentive to the emotional ebb and flow of the match. Each player needs to be stroked at times, challenged at times, and at other times left completely alone. Part of winning, from a player's point of view, is understanding the moment-by-moment needs of your teammates and acquiring the interpersonal skills to meet those needs when they arise during competition. This player had become so locked into the pursuit of her individual goal to increase her hitting efficiency that she distanced herself from her teammates and became a drain on the team's energy.

I am not in any way saying that individual goals are not important. I am pointing out, however, that a coach must be vigilant to detect when and where individual and team goals conflict. When this occurs, team goals must take priority. In this particular case, I withdrew my emphasis on improving the player's hitting percentage and began stressing with her the sensitivities required to maintain a solid team chemistry during competition. Her hitting percentage took a bit of a dip, but we began playing much better as a team.

Outcome Versus Performance Goals

I break ranks to some degree with the sport psychologists on this question. Most of what I have read and heard from this group says that our attention in goal setting should be aimed at setting performance standards, not at winning or losing. Winning and losing, they argue, involve too many variables that are beyond our control. We can control only our own performance, they say, and it is within this realm that we should confine our goal-setting activities.

I don't agree. Competition in team sports is defined as the striving by two opponents for the prize of *winning*. There is nothing wrong with this basic fact. I believe competing is a noble enterprise that teaches us, if we conduct ourselves according to the principles of class and integrity, to win and lose with style. To establish goals that feature anything short of winning is to do a disservice to the athletes who compete for us. The timetable for winning may vary. A coach may decide a team is too young or insufficiently talented to win right away and may devise a 5-year plan that calls for developmental activities first and winning later. But winning matches has to be the centerpiece of the team's goal structure.

Furthermore, the goal of winning (focusing on outcome rather than on performance) acts as a catalyst in synthesizing all of our preparation as a team. It is the one thing that unites us all at the same time and place. It is the magnet that pulls together all of the different paths each of us has followed to arrive at the competition. It is, in my judgment, a necessary condition for becoming a winning program. To focus only on performance goals is to draw attention away from the fundamental reason the team exists. I have seen many examples of this. I have heard coaches tell their teams something like this: Tonight our goal is to attack with a .310 efficiency, pass 2.45, and serve with a 1:1 ace-to-error ratio. No one can tell me that these types of goals motivate a team to go out and *beat* their opponent. They are excellent standards for measuring how well a team performs over time. But when elevated to the status of goals, they fall short of programming a team to seek victories—and this is what a team should be striving to do in competitive, varsity athletics.

Selecting the Goal

Years ago, having arrived early for a practice session at the arena where we were to compete later that evening, I paid a visit to the office of a longtime coaching friend. He wasn't in, but the door to his office was open. I walked in and took a seat, waiting for him to return. On a blackboard behind his desk was written, "Seasonal Goal: Win the Conference Championship." I was dumbfounded. There was no way in the world my friend's team could win any kind of championship. They were traditionally near the bottom of the standings from year to year and did not possess much talent. I would like to have seen his players' reactions when they heard him announce that their goal was to win the conference championship.

Goals cannot be plucked from the air. They must be determined on the basis of a rational process. It is imperative that you, the coach, accurately assess your own competitive arena to determine what is possible and what is not. This involves several things. First, you must undertake a preseason assessment of your own team's capabilities, weaknesses, emotional stability, work ethic, and level of commitment. You must also evaluate the same qualities in each of your opponents, one by one. How many players have each of them lost to graduation? Are any of their new players capable of contributing immediately? Which teams are in an upswing? Which are on a decline? Which arenas are difficult to win in? Which teams do you typically have a tough time playing against? Analyze every variable, go over your schedule, and decide which teams you think you have a chance to beat.

Pushing the Edge

Now you are ready to begin formulating your seasonal goals. At this point, it is time to apply a principle I call "pushing the edge." This involves setting goals that are on the far edge of the realm of *possibility*. It is a mistake, as in my friend's case, to set unrealistic goals. But it is an even bigger mistake to set goals that fall short of players' expectations of what they *can* accomplish. Through your own analysis, identify the range of possibilities for your team's performance. Then go to the far edge of that range, and that's where you set your goals. Your team will always feel challenged, yet they will never be forced to experience the demoralizing effect of knowing intuitively that they have been asked to achieve goals that are simply out of their reach.

Goal Peaks

It is also important to establish goal peaks for the season. Out of 32 matches in the collegiate season, I figure that my teams will usually play 6 great matches, 6 bad ones, and the rest will be somewhere in between. It would be unusual to find a team that plays near the top of their potential every time out. This means that I can't set goals that require my team to be great all the time. I must select certain peaks, usually three or four, during the season when I would like my team to be playing their best volleyball. These peaks differ from season to season. There may be an early-season tournament or a particular opponent that I want my team to be ready for. And then I want them "up" again for a stretch of key Big Ten matches. And, of course, we always try to peak for the critical NCAA tournament matches at the end of the season. You have to cross your fingers and hope that you survive the nonpeak matches. Sometimes you don't, and this is why you see so many teams look great in beating a quality opponent and then look terrible 1 week later in dropping a match to a weaker team. But peaking is a fact of life in team sports, and the wise coach attempts to find ways to harness its power.

Climbing the Rungs of the Ladder

My last point on goal selection has to do with the concept of "rungs in the ladder." It is very difficult to skip too many rungs at one time as you design your 3-to-5-year plan. This is why, in planning the Illinois program, I set goals each year that exceeded the previous year's goals by only one or two rungs. When we lost in the NCAA regional semifinal in 1985, we set a goal to advance to the regional finals the next year. And when we lost in the regional final in 1986, we vowed to win the regional championship in 1987. These last rungs are very difficult to climb, and it would be a mistake to set goals that call for skipping one. Occasionally this will happen; a team can have a Cinderella year, as we did in 1985. But overall, programs tend to improve one rung at a time. Coaches need to be careful not to be swept up in the emotional enthusiasm that can be present in goal-setting meetings. Plan your climb to the top one rung at a time.

Goal Articulation

Sometimes it is not only what goals you select, but how they are articulated that can make the difference in whether or not they are accomplished. This is a subtle, and not often talked about, skill in goal setting. I offered the example of Don Hardin's use of the word *clinch* to articulate the fact that we wanted to win the Big Ten championship in 1986. Let me give you one more example.

In 1989 Illinois had to go to Nebraska for a dual match late in the season. Illinois and Nebraska had become rivals and had been considered for years to be the two best teams in the Mideast region. I knew that we were in for a tough test against one of the nation's best teams and on their home floor. On top of all this, Terry Pettit, their head coach, told me that the match would be scheduled for 5:00 p.m. so that fans leaving the home football game—which, by the way, was located only a few hundred yards from the volleyball arena—could simply walk across the parking lot and come to the volleyball match. He knew this was a big match and was pumping up as much support as he could. And I knew that we had little chance of beating Nebraska under these circumstances unless I found a way to capture my team's imagination and instill in them the belief that they *could* pull off the win.

One of our goals for the 1989 season, therefore, was the "Ambush in Lincoln." This had a great ring to it. We were going out west to cowboy country, and the word *ambush* sort of fit. But even more importantly, *ambush* implied that we were secretly organizing a surprise attack. It allowed us to think of ourselves as the wily invaders and Nebraska as the surprised victims of our attack.

It worked. We won an extremely close match in front of over 5,000 fans. And I am convinced that without *ambush*, it would not have happened in quite the same fashion. Goals must be articulated in such a way that they create extra motivation, capture the team's fancy, and strike the right nerve. It is one more skill in goal setting that can make the difference.

Goal Environment

The environment in which goals are pursued determines, to a great extent, whether or not those goals will be achieved. It would be extremely difficult, for example, for a team to decide it wants to win a conference championship, and then be subjected to inadequate practice facilities, aloof administrators, inferior equipment, and negative-thinking coaches. The coach must set goals for and with the team, but this isn't the end of the process. After goals are set, the coach must begin the arduous process of preparing the environment within which these goals will be pursued.

Every component of the program must be examined for its potential impact on the attitude of the players. The environment must constantly say to the players, We support you in your goals. Early in my tenure at Illinois, I worked hard to establish a practice situation that would be secure and free from distraction. I saw to it that the equipment—balls, nets, standards, and such—was of the best quality. I also decided to outfit players in stylish practice uniforms as one more way to enhance self-esteem on a daily basis. I lobbied constantly with all available support personnel, such as trainers, sports information staff, maintenance workers, business office people, and other key administrative agencies, to treat my program with respect and to expect the same in return. The struggle for respect, the effort to restructure the players' environment consumed at least as much of my time during the first few years as did coaching the team. But it was no less important on my list of priorities.

My efforts to generate positive expectations in the community outside the collegiate environment were extensive also. This population included local residents of Champaign, Urbana, and surrounding towns (I like to think of them all as potential volleyball fans), high school and USVBA junior coaches from around the region, local and national volleyball media representatives, and anyone else I could get to listen to my pitch.

One of my first moves in 1983 was to begin chipping away at the negative perceptions of the University of Illinois volleyball program held by many in the critical recruiting area around Chicago. I held a clinic entitled *Inside Illini Volleyball* at one of the suburban hotels in an attempt to showcase the new commitment Illinois had made to its volleyball program and to provide an opportunity for people to get to know me and my staff. I made it a point to be at every high school and USVBA junior tournament possible, always wearing my Illinois garb and talking nonstop about how Illinois would soon be a force in midwestern volleyball. I spoke to every local civic group who would have me, telling them about how exciting this new sport and this new team were going to be. I made bold claims to the press, forecasting that Illinois would challenge for a Big Ten championship within 3 years. I was energetic and cocky, and I believed what I was saying. I was paving the way for the success that was to come. I was working nonstop to create an environment that would reinforce the goal strategies that I was refining with my players.

Wrap-up

Looking back, I don't think I ever stopped to wonder what would happen, how big a fool I would look if the team did not become a winner. Failing never occurred to me. Fortunately, by the time the team started to win big in 1985, my calculations proved to be correct. My players became community celebrities. We began to regularly sell out ancient Kenney Gym for home matches. Local and national media began to feature Illinois volleyball prominently in both electronic and print outlets. Blue-chip recruits were drawn to the program. Our support personnel began to point with pride to the fact that they were associated with our team. The players were doing well in the classroom, and the faculty began to adopt them as model student athletes. We were on our way. But none of this was an accident. It was the planned result of an elaborate strategy aimed at structuring the expectations within the environment in which my program was to evolve.

Concepts in
Program Structuring

Two programs can have the same goals. Both may declare that they want to win the conference championship. Several factors determine which of the two will succeed.

PROGRAM PHILOSOPHY

One of these factors has to do with the manner in which the overall program is structured. The team that provides the better, more productive experience—everything else being equal—will probably come out the winner.

The Learning Environment

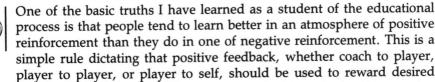

One of the basic truths I have learned as a student of the educational process is that people tend to learn better in an atmosphere of positive reinforcement than they do in one of negative reinforcement. This is a simple rule dictating that positive feedback, whether coach to player, player to player, or player to self, should be used to reward desired behavior. Negative feedback only retards the learning process.

The rule of positive feedback does not mean that all feedback must be sugar-coated or that there is no room for criticism. It means that positive feedback should be present whenever the desired behavior is produced. When the desired behavior is not produced the feedback can be corrective, as in "Keep your elbow higher as you finish your armswing." But negative feedback, such as "No, no, no . . . you'll never become an outside hitter with an armswing like that!" should be avoided. Nor does it mean that positive feedback should be administered when it is not deserved. Don't say, Nice job, if it wasn't. Positive feedback is a reward system intended to encourage good performance, not a device to soothe an athlete's emotional state. It does mean that players must feel that they are functioning in an environment that, taken as a whole, rewards them when they are producing behaviors that enhance their pursuit of designated goals.

The primary method of providing positive feedback is through verbal exchanges. Coaches need to become skilled at catching players doing things right and then immediately telling them that what they've done is correct. "That's a good job of keeping your elbow high through your armswing," "Nice pass," and "I like the way you bounced back from that earlier mistake" are all examples of verbal, positive reinforcement.

Other methods can be effective as well. I like to hold frequent competitions during practice sessions, for example, and record the results on a daily basis. One day we might hold a serving competition; the next day, a triples tournament; and then a six-on-six gamelike drill the following day. At the end of the week, I total everyone's cumulative scores from each of the competitions, and the overall winner is awarded a special practice jersey to be worn during the following week's practice sessions. This may sound corny to some, but the jersey has become a symbol of achievement and is one more visible sign that players will be positively rewarded when they perform at a high level.

Furthermore, a coach has to understand that athletes must feel free to make errors. I didn't say that they should be coddled and encouraged to make errors. But a player must be able to perform without being afraid of making a mistake. You've heard the old line that teams sometimes play "not to lose" instead of playing to win. The former is often the result of a team's being reared in a learning environment where negative reinforcement predominates. Players are afraid of making mistakes. The latter is more often the product of a coach who understands that mistakes are a necessary part of the trial-and-error enterprise and that it is more productive to reward successes when they occur than to magnify and dwell on mistakes.

Coaches must also develop pedagogical consistency. If you have designed a particular course of learning for a drill, a practice session, or a training phase, then make sure you stay on that course. It can be extremely confusing and frustrating for your players if you send mixed messages. If you set up a blocking drill, for example, emphasizing proper hand position, then your feedback during that drill should be directed exclusively to hand position. Even if you spot other deficiencies, you should resist the urge to correct every problem as it occurs. I once observed a coach who all week during practice told his players to work on hard, tough serving, because their weekend opponent was a good passing team and he felt his team had to take some risks at the service line to win the match. Serve tough, he told them, even if it means you'll probably commit more serving errors than normal. As the match began, his players committed six errors in their first seven service attempts. The coach called a time-out and screamed at the team for making all those errors. Needless to say, his players became extremely confused by his sudden change of course. They served poorly the rest of the night and ended up losing the match.

Interpersonal Skill Acquisition

It is a responsibility of everyone in the program, coaches and players alike, to acquire the skills necessary to successfully negotiate the conflicts that inevitably arise within the team setting. A team is a close-knit collection of individuals asked to interact with one another on an intimate and daily basis, and often in an environment loaded with stress and pressure. Each individual is literally forced by circumstance to engage in these interactions. It is not a matter of choice. The presence of sound, interpersonal skills on everyone's part can play an important role in achieving team goals. Poor interpersonal skills can spell disaster.

Givers Versus Takers

One popular way to think about this issue is to evaluate each individual according to the giver-versus-taker spectrum. Anyone who has ever played a team sport knows that there are some athletes who are givers and some who are takers. Givers are players who make everyone around them perform better. They take care of their own assignment on the court. But they also have enough energy left over to provide a pat on the back to a demoralized teammate, to dish out positive reinforcement whenever a teammate makes a good play, and to be a constant source of inspiration when the team is in need of a lift. Takers are just the opposite. They are sponges that soak up everyone's energies. They need consoling after mistakes. They complain in the locker room about every little frustration. They rarely extend a hand to assist a teammate in need. They are often in the center of team controversies. In short, they are a drain on the team. The giver has developed the interpersonal skills required to function successfully in a team setting. The taker has developed very few of these skills. Everyone can be plotted somewhere along this spectrum, and it is a good, shorthand way of assessing an individual's interpersonal skill level.

Personality Patterns

I consider these skills so critical to team success that I decided to seek the expertise of a professional. I was introduced to Kay McGuire, who directs the Center for Creative Communication in Urbana, Illinois. By the use of a few brief but amazingly accurate diagnostic instruments, she was able to classify each player and staff member according to four classical personality styles. Behavior patterns among individuals from the same personality style are remarkably consistent. Most people exhibit a combination of two or more of these, but one style usually dominates—particularly when that person is under stress. Knowing which classical pattern to link up with each athlete and coach, and thereby knowing what behavior to expect from that individual and how to maximize the probability of interacting successfully with them in the team environment, has been an enormous boost in my continuing effort to improve our interpersonal skills.

I am not going to attempt a detailed explanation of these classical patterns. Instead, I will provide an example of how this particular theoretical perspective has helped me handle my team. Throughout my career I have motivated my teams by telling them things that I think would motivate me. But sometimes I finish what I think is a great motivational speech, and all I see are blank faces staring back at me. This occurred frequently with my 1989 team, and it was through my work with Kay that I began to understand why it was happening.

I tend to appeal to the emotions when I motivate. When I was an athlete, I would get charged up whenever a coach would say to me something like "You made a commitment to this team, now go out there and show me some character!" I always assumed that everyone else would be similarly affected. After all, if you make a commitment, you have to do everything possible to deliver on that commitment. If you fail, everyone will notice and will lose their respect for you. And this would be devastating. I feel this way because, according to my particular classical pattern, I live a creative, expressive, and risk-taking lifestyle. My identity is measured by my ability to pull off the various schemes that are always percolating in my mind. To challenge my self-esteem by questioning my commitment to goals strikes me to the very core.

But this is definitely *not* true for everyone. In time-outs with my 1989 team, I found myself saying, The reason you're playing poorly right now is that you've forgotten the fact that you committed yourself to certain goals . . . . You need to dig down deep and remotivate yourself to perform. Heads turned away, eyes stared at the floor. I was having no impact on my players with this line of thought.

Kay helped me to understand that my 1989 roster was inhabited by an unusually large number of individuals who reflected a very different classical pattern than mine. They were, for lack of a better term, perfectionists. They were extremely task-oriented under pressure and preferred to operate in an environment free of what they considered emotional clutter. Their obsession with perfection meant that their confidence came from having rehearsed their tasks over and over before being called on to perform them. When under pressure, they needed to be reminded that they could, in fact, perform well, because they had practiced and succeeded in performing these same skills many times in the past. Appealing to their emotions was not only irrelevant to them, it was a distraction. Instead, they needed to be told, in a simple and straightforward, informational fashion, what I wanted them to do on the court immediately after the time-out. They needed to be reminded of proper passing technique, of who should go where in the offensive pattern, and so on. To me, what to do next was obvious. It was the emotional fire that had to be rekindled. But to my perfectionists, the call for renewed emotional commitment was just as obvious. To them, the simple passing along of step-by-step instructions outlining how to win the next side-out was of paramount importance and would have held them spellbound. Once I understood this, my communication skills during time-outs improved significantly.

This has been one of hundreds of similar experiences in our program over the past year, which have taught me the value of learning as much as possible about the interactional process within a team setting. We have not solved all of our problems, and there are new ones popping up all the time. But we have begun to build a base of knowledge and have acquired at least the minimal skills to feel confident that we can function efficiently as a group while we pursue our goals. I feel safe in saying that the acquisition of skills for creating successful interpersonal relationships should be high on the list of priorities of any coach hoping to build a winning program.

Accountability Versus Rules

When people ask me to talk about my philosophy of coaching, I always include the following item. It is very important, in my estimation of things, to transfer the burden of responsibility for achieving goals from the coach to the players as soon as possible. All of us in coaching know that our players will succeed only if they live according to certain principles of honesty, fair play, self-discipline, and so on. And in an attempt to get players to abide by these principles, many coaches write out a set of team rules and distribute them. The coach is the boss, the rules are to be followed, and the player gets into trouble if the rules are broken.

This makes me uncomfortable. Once an athlete decides to play for me, I make it clear that she has bought into a very basic agreement. I will perform my obligations as a coach, and she will perform hers as a player. It is her responsibility to live up to her end of the bargain, not mine. If I give her a list of rules to follow and put myself in the position of having to monitor her behavior and discipline her if she breaks them, then it seems to me that I'm doing all the work to see that the bargain is kept. This is the problem with rules. The coach is forced to carry the burden of responsibility for both parties.

I prefer to teach my players the overall concept of accountability. They face hundreds of choices every day: whether or not to make their beds before they leave their rooms in the morning, whether to use the half hour after lunch to study or to nap, whether or not to go all out in the conditioning sprints at the end of practice, and so on. I emphasize the nurturing of skills for making good decisions, decisions that will advance them one step further on the road toward accomplishing their goals. Gradually, I try to bring each player along to the point where she accepts the responsibility for captaining her own ship. This is sometimes a lengthy process. But I prefer to coach athletes who are mature enough to understand on their own what has to be done to accomplish goals and are prepared to develop the discipline to do it. This is what I mean by accountability, and it is a much more productive process than riding herd over players by means of a set of rules.

The box that follows lists some guidelines from our Player Accountability Program. Notice that I do not tell my athletes what to do. I attempt to teach them how to focus their perceptions of situations so they can make choices that are in line with the goals that we have established together for the program. We approach virtually every issue in this fashion. The players sometimes resist this format and want to return to an easier player/coach relationship in which they don't have to do much thinking. It is sometimes easier to obey than to live through the trial-and-error pain that accompanies the learning of responsibility. But I never yield on this issue. I am convinced that player accountability is essential to creating a winning environment.

There are certainly many more pertinent things to say about how to structure the program environment so that goals can be achieved more effectively. But the three items highlighted here, learning environment,

---

Player Accountability Program

1. Develop a mental plan. Establish personal and competitive goals. Develop a lifestyle that reflects the pursuit of these goals. Don't say you want to be a champion and then exhibit poor time management skills, poor rest and nutritional habits, sloppy personal habits, or questionable social behavior in your daily life.

2. Solve the motivation issue. Don't put a coach in the awkward position of making you do the things you have already committed yourself to do. This means trying your best in all drills, scrimmages, and physical conditioning sessions. This means ridding yourself of the many distractions (conflicts with teammates, a low exam score, a bad day, or boyfriend problems) that can prevent your being properly motivated. Be responsible for pushing yourself beyond your comfort zone as often as possible.

3. Learn the *line of wisdom* with regard to social behavior. Every social situation, especially on college campuses, is filled with difficult choices. The decision to behave in a particular fashion may be acceptable in one situation but unwise in another. Refine your sense of right and wrong as a student athlete and learn how to creatively apply it in social situations.

---

interpersonal skill acquisition, and the emphasis on accountability, go a long way in describing my approach to this task. I have logged many experiences over the years that confirm in my own mind that I am on the right path. But the most vivid I can relate to you occurred in 1983, just after my first Illinois team had turned in the worst seasonal win-loss record of my career.

During a series of routine postseason, individual player meetings, one of my athletes told me that being on this team had been the most positive experience of her life. Think about it. We had just finished 5-25. How positive could this have been for anyone? But she explained that the win-loss record was meaningless compared to the self-discipline and goal-pursuing skills she had learned by being part of the team. I knew then, as I know now, that these skills are at the heart of any successful human venture. They will always be a central part of my efforts to build a winning volleyball program.

Team Chemistry

Every coach of a team sport has at one time or another talked about the importance of team chemistry, how well the players mesh in a psychological sense. But what exactly goes into making a good team chemistry, and how do you teach it to your team? This is a question Don Hardin and I addressed during our early years together at Illinois.

We made it a point to watch good volleyball teams as often as possible. We watched dual matches, conference championships, NCAA Final Four matches, and top international matches. Our goal was to figure out why certain teams were winning consistently and, specifically, what role each player performed in creating a winning chemistry.

Stud

Don came up with this term. Every great team, he reasoned, has one player on the roster who everyone considers a "stud." This player usually possesses superior talent and plays a dominant offensive or defensive role in the team's system. In volleyball, the stud often plays the middle blocker position. In basketball, they are centers; in football, they are usually quarterbacks; and in baseball, they are either pitchers or hitters. Some common examples are Kareem Abdul-Jabbar, Dwight Gooden, Joe Montana, and Babe Ruth. In the sport of volleyball, Lang Ping, Steve Timmons, Tara Cross, and Tee Williams come to mind. Everyone, including any opponent, knows that the stud can take control of the game at any time. The mere presence of a stud gives a team a tremendous psychological edge. Studs may be short on other attributes, but they are physically intimidating.

Winner

It was obvious to us both as we compared notes that every great team was blessed with at least one all-out winner. A winner is a player who never *ever* contemplates the possibility of losing. No matter what the circumstances, no matter how low the score, no matter how much bad fortune has come their way, winners play every point as if they have a chance to win the match. Larry Bird and Magic Johnson are two athletes who come to mind. Mary Eggers is another. These players are courageous and are constantly taking risks. They lay themselves on the line at every stage of a competition. Their commitment to winning is infectious, and they often carry the entire emotional load of their team. They make everyone around them better players. They are a rare breed. If you ever find one, make sure you find a way to put a winner on your team.

Stabilizer

We had a more difficult time identifying this particular role. Most athletes are not sufficiently skilled to be studs or psychologically equipped to be winners. Yet championship teams are heavily populated with players who fit neither of these roles. What psychological function, then, do these players perform? We concluded that they act as stabilizers. They are usually low-error players who are seldom the primary reason your team wins, but never the reason it loses. They are traditionally referred to by coaches and sports commentators as role players. They set the stage so the headliners, the studs and winners, can function.

Placing the Three Types of Players in a Lineup

There you have it: stud, winner, and stabilizer. These are the three fundamental ingredients for a successful team chemistry. I have applied this analysis to every championship team in every sport, and it never fails. These three elements will always be found. But they must be blended together in the right way or the chemistry can go bad. This is where the coach must make some important decisions.

Studs are hard to find. Not many players possess this kind of talent, and it would be unusual for a coach to ever have more than one on the roster at any given time. This is a good thing, because there is not enough room on the court for more than one. They are frequently temperamental, thriving on the attention they receive and bothered when they have to share top billing. This is not a criticism of this type of player. In fact, surviving the pressures of playing the stud role probably requires an eccentric personality. So as you begin to blend the ingredients together for a championship chemistry, don't make the mistake of trying to put more than one stud in your starting lineup.

Winners, on the other hand, don't suffer from this affliction. They would prefer that everyone plunge into the fray with the same banzai attitude that they themselves possess. But they also know how to maintain a winning attitude even when teammates begin to wilt. If you can locate a winner for every position, do so. It's impossible to have too many of them on your roster. But in reality, the possibility of this is the same as for studs. There aren't very many of them available.

I'd like to say one more thing about winners: Try to find one to be your setter. It is to a team's advantage that the person who handles the ball the most and who runs the offense be a winner. In volleyball, this means the setter. In basketball, it is the point guard; in football, the quarterback; and in baseball, the catcher. In selecting a setter, I believe the winner quality is at least as important as skill level. A winner in the setter's position can have a dramatic impact on your team.

As you piece together your lineup, which is fortunate enough to have a stud middle blocker and a winner for a setter, pay careful attention to the selection of the remaining starting players. Ability is only one criterion. Each athlete should also be evaluated according to his or her potential impact on the team's chemistry. If players cannot perform as studs or winners, they must be able to contribute as stabilizers. Let me give you an example.

You have a choice to make between two outside hitters for the final spot in your lineup. One is a great athlete who can rip the ball from the outside. She is full of potential, and everyone agrees that she will be a great player some day. But she makes a number of hitting errors and is an inconsistent passer. Sometimes her mistakes become a real source of distraction to her teammates. Furthermore, she is a bit moody and unpredictable in terms of her emotional contribution to the team. The other player possesses only average ability and cannot make some of the dramatic plays the first hitter can make. But she rarely makes unforced errors and is extremely reliable. She is a levelheaded competitor and is supportive of herself and her teammates during matches. She exudes confidence. Many coaches would go with the more talented athlete, and they would be making a mistake. I recommend starting the less talented athlete, who can add stability to the team's chemistry.

Another way of evaluating your personnel is to list the three categories—stud, winner, and stabilizer—and rank each of your players according to ability in each category. Table 6.1 gives a hypothetical case.

Gail, my middle blocker, is in the correct position. She has tremendous physical ability and enjoys playing the stud role for my team. She has average tendencies as a winner. And the fact that she is up and down a bit in her performance and therefore does not provide stability to my lineup does not bother me. I don't expect her to be a stabilizer.

Sally is my setter, and she, too, is in the correct position. It doesn't matter that she doesn't rank very high on the stud scale. She is a winner and contributes to the team's stability.

I also start Sara as an outside hitter. Sara has decent talent, as can be seen by her ranking in the stud column. And even though she is not seen as a winner, she is perceived as the most reliable, dependable stabilizer on the team. I look to others to generate a winning attitude, not to Sara.

Table 6.1 Rank of Players by Effectiveness in Role

Range of Ability	Role		
	Stud	Winner	Stabilizer
High	Gail	Sally	Sara
	Lori	Lori	Bev
	Deirdre	Bev	Sally
	Sara	Joey	Pam
	Donna	Gail	Joey
	Pam	Jeanne	Lori
	Bev	Deirdre	Jeanne
	Joey	Pam	Deirdre
	Sally	Donna	Gail
Low	Jeanne	Sara	Donna

And then, of course, every team has a Donna. Donna has good athletic ability, but not good enough to be a candidate for the stud role. She is at or near the bottom on both the winner and stabilizer categories. The fact is that regardless of the outward appearance of being a good volleyball player, she provides none of the three essential chemistry ingredients and therefore is not a good candidate for a starting position.

The point here is that as you build your roster, one of the most important tasks ahead of you is to attract and blend the right mix of players. This insight will have far-reaching implications for recruiting decisions, practice planning, staff hiring, lineup selection, and substitution patterns during matches. Athletic ability and skill level are important. But of equal importance are the chemistry-related attributes each player brings to the program.

PROGRAM ADMINISTRATION

I can remember the 30-minute drive from my high school teaching job to the practice gym at the University of Pittsburgh. It was during those 30 minutes that I handled most of the administrative tasks pertaining to my volleyball program. It was simply a matter of telling myself what needed to be done that day. I had no office. I did all of my volleyball-related paperwork while sitting on the steps outside the women's athletics reception area. I had a part-time assistant coach, who drove even further to and from practice than I did, and we saw each other only during practice hours. Recruiting was merely a matter of contacting local kids whenever I found the time to do it. I shared a secretary with all of the other coaches and ended up typing most of my own correspondence, preparing my own expense reports, and keeping my own files. I rarely came into contact with administrators. There were no large crowds, no press, and no event management personnel. I set up my own nets, swept the floor, and ran my own promotions campaign by preparing flyers for my players to spread around campus. At that time, my program, like most others, was a skeleton operation made up of a part-time staff, a small budget, and a roster of players. There was no real need for an elaborate administrative plan.

Administrative Role at Illinois

But times have changed. Let me highlight for you some of the features of the current University of Illinois volleyball program:

I now direct a staff of 4 (1 full-time head coach, 2 full-time assistants, and 1 graduate assistant).

Matches have become major events, requiring a full-scale event management team. I was stunned one evening when an opposing coach walked over to me before a match and told me that he had counted a total of 73 support personnel working at the site. This included parking lot attendants, security police, ushers, program sellers, concessionaires, sports information personnel, statisticians, team managers, maintenance workers, administrators, officials, ball shaggers, equipment supervisors, and so on.

Press and public-speaking responsibilities have escalated to become a major drain on the weekly schedule. During 1 week of a recent season, I gave a total of 24 interviews. There have been as many as 47 press credentials issued for an NCAA play-off match at Kenney Gym. We have held regular press conferences, attended by newspaper, radio, and television representatives for the past 5 years. During that same period, all of our matches, at home and away, have been broadcast live on radio station WHMS in Champaign. This includes a regular coaches' show and live interviews with players. Coaches and players alike are responsible for fulfilling an elaborate schedule of personal appearances and public-speaking engagements within the community.

The support network for servicing athletes' needs and enhancing their performance has become diverse. We provide specialized programs in academic services, nutrition, sports vision enhancement, interpersonal skills training, stress management, and personal wellness evaluation. We conduct a player education program that covers these issues, as well as others, such as alcohol and substance abuse, statistical analysis in volleyball, and injury prevention.

The administrative infrastructure has grown considerably. I now interact constantly with athletic directors, assistants to athletic directors, business office personnel, sports information directors, medical staff, academic liaisons, and the like.

Where there were only a handful of stalwart volleyball fans in Pittsburgh in 1976, I now have the luxury of working with the 500 members of the Networkers, the official support group for Fighting Illini volleyball. This means attending board meetings and social functions, and fulfilling the various needs of a booster organization. We also have been rated, in terms of average attendance, among the top three programs nationally over the past 5 years. The responsibilities associated with sustaining this fan interest have become substantial.

Budget management has turned into a complicated exercise. Take the travel budget for example. In 1976 my players slept 4 to a room in motels, packed themselves into vans for 10- to 12-hour trips, and ate on strict dollar allowances. Now we stay in better hotels with 2 to a room. We sometimes arrange charter flights to and from matches. We eat a nutritionally sound diet while we're on the road. And we travel with a greatly expanded party, which includes a sports information director, a team manager, a play-by-play radio announcer, and a trainer—in addition to 12 players and 4 coaches. The budget also includes line items for scouting and coaches' professional travel. Recruiting, an item that was nonexistent during my first 4 years of budget management, has now become a major component in program expenditures. Occasional review and cross-checking have been replaced by frequent and thorough audit of all budgetary transactions, the mode of operation in managing today's collegiate volleyball budgets.

Equipment concerns have also evolved to new levels of sophistication. In the old days, when equipment budgets were miniscule, jerseys and warm-ups had to be cheap and had to last 2 to 3 years, perhaps more. Athletes were allowed no more than one pair of shoes per year. After that, they had to buy their own. Equipment concerns were simple and straightforward. Now I negotiate and administer elaborate contracts with suppliers of apparel, shoes, bags, and balls. Agents of commercial products are coming to us, asking for the privilege of supplying our equipment needs. This certainly softens the blow to the annual equipment budget. But it significantly increases the amount of administrative time devoted to securing and maintaining sound relationships with commercial sponsors.

Compliance with conference and NCAA legislation now consumes an inordinate amount of staff time. When I first started coaching, I barely knew these rules existed. Very little emphasis was placed on learning them. We had real problems to solve, such as getting practice time, finding affordable ways to honor our travel commitments, locating enough chairs to set out for team benches at home matches, and finding someone sympathetic enough to our sport to allow our athletes workout time in the weight room. Today the climate has completely changed. Rules compliance has become a major item on everyone's agenda. The rules are, at best, conflicting, inconsistent, and virtually impossible to digest. But we all spend a great deal of time trying to teach our staff and players how to comply with them.

And we now have a professional association, the American Volleyball Coaches Association, which also asks for a portion of our administrative time. This is a responsibility I gladly shoulder. At last, we have an organization that serves as an advocate for the concerns of our sport, a voice to speak on our behalf. When we are asked to serve on a committee or fill out and return a survey, we do so out of a commitment to the future of our sport and our profession, even though it adds to the administrative load on our respective programs.

And, for a growing number of coaches, a portion of our time is devoted to working with the USVBA's Coaching Accreditation Program (CAP). I enlisted in 1988 to become part of the charter CAP cadre. We instruct at clinics, prepare educational materials, and assist in the structuring of the content for each of the five levels of accreditation available through CAP. This program is indispensable if we are to achieve national standards for preparing and evaluating volleyball coaches.

Thirty minutes a day is no longer enough time to devote to program administration. It has become a full-time job, requiring detailed and elaborate planning.

Five-Year Plan

It is imperative that a coach construct a 5-year plan that reflects the performance goals established for the program. This plan serves as the structural and chronological blueprint by which the program is pieced together. Step 1 is to identify each program component important to achieving team goals. Step 2 is to assess where each component stands, where it ought to be by year 5 of the plan, and what year-by-year incremental advances need to be implemented in order to get it there. Step 3 is to design and graphically portray the plan using a chart-type format, so it can be viewed as one, integrated, harmonious enterprise.

During my first season at Illinois, on October 21, 1983, I wrote the following introduction to my initial 5-year plan proposal:

For some time now, I have been taking a close look at the volleyball environment (local, state, conference, regional, and national) within which I am working, so that I can make some decisions about what I will need to produce the level of program you [Dr. Karol Kahrs, director of Women's Athletics] are looking for. And let me be specific about this . . . it is my clear understanding that you are seeking a team that can contend for the national championship, that you brought me here to accomplish that task, and that volleyball has been elevated to join women's basketball as a priority sport at the University of Illinois. The recommendations that follow are drawn from my perceptions of what will be needed in order to accomplish this goal. I want to emphasize that I think it is important not to view these recommendations in comparison to what other programs may or may not have, but rather as items that are needed based on the specific circumstances within which the University of Illinois volleyball program must compete and recruit. And finally, it is important that we avoid the pitfall of doing just enough to "stay even" with our competitors. We are significantly behind right now. We must catch up and pass. This means we have to build a program that offers more than our competitors on a conference, regional, and then a national level. In some ways we may have to be pioneers in building a women's volleyball program.

In Table 6.2, I have reproduced the essential features of the 1984-1988 5-Year Plan to build the University of Illinois volleyball program. Like all such plans, some components were conceived with too little patience and others without sufficient aggressiveness. But on the whole, this was the original blueprint for moving the Illinois team from last place in the Big Ten in 1983 to two consecutive Final Four appearances in 1987 and 1988.

Administrative Style

How a plan is implemented can be just as important as the plan itself. I am referring to the role that administrative style plays in the degree to which a staff succeeds in accomplishing its goals. Head coaches must know Xs and Os. But they must also know how to manage a staff and how to preside over the entire spectrum of activities that make up today's athletic programs. I suggest three fundamental administrative concepts that can go a long way to enhance a head coach's skills in this area.

Table 6.2   University of Illinois Five-Year Volleyball Plan

Item	1984-85	1985-86	1986-87	1987-88	1988-89
Staff	Add graduate assistant coach	Add event manager	Office space for expanded staff; 3 managers	Add second assistant coach	Two full-time assistants, 1 graduate assistant, 3 managers
Facilities	Adequate practice time for traditional and nontraditional seasons	Improve event environment: bleachers, PA system, lighting, etc.	Resurface floor of Kenney Gym		Prepare to relocate to new facility
Program goals	Top four in Big 10	Top two in Big 10; at-large NCAA bid	Win Big 10; NCAA bid, Top-Twenty national ranking	Win Big 10; regional championship; final four	Win Big 10; regional championship; win national championship
In-season scheduling	Sponsor Illini Classic; increase guarantee budget	Schedule four top-twenty teams; bring in 1 or 2 top teams	Maximize number of top-twenty teams in nonconference schedule	Maintain elite schedule	Maintain elite schedule
Off-season scheduling	International tour in spring	Compete in maximum allowable tournaments	Maximum competition	International tour in spring	Maximum competition

146

Radio and TV		Selected live radio broadcasts	Negotiate radio contact to broadcast all matches (live); seek TV broadcast	Maintain radio broadcast schedule; maintain and expand TV	Maintain radio broadcast schedule; maintain and expand TV
Team travel	Eliminate staff driving	Increase budget to include more in travel party—sports information direction; manager; additional assistant coach	Maintain travel party of 19		
Equipment	Expand and upgrade inventory	Seek commercial shoe and apparel contracts	Seek ball contract; maintain other contracts	Maintain contracts; upgrade video equip.	Maintain contracts
Coaches' travel	All staff to NCAA championship and convention; at least one major clinic per coach	Pursue USA national program coaching assignments	Maintain and enhance	Maintain and enhance	Maintain and enhance

(Continued)

Table 6.2 (Continued)

Item	1984-85	1985-86	1986-87	1987-88	1988-89
Booster organization	Coordinate initial organizational meetings; begin newsletter	Solidify organizational structure; banquet sponsorship; membership plan	Increase membership	Continue support efforts	Continue support efforts
Recruiting	Recruit 3 top players from elite pool; recruit 2 walk-ons; seek major budget increase	Recruit 3 top players; increase budget; develop national recruiting network	Recruit 3 top players; computerize recruiting strategies	Recruit 3 top players; hire full-time recruiting assistant	Recruit 3 top players
Promotion	Budget to initiate promotional plan for volleyball; clinic for Illinois high school coaches	Attendance goals; set Big 10 record; match promotion plan; advertising plan	Season ticket plan; seek speaking engagements, appearances	Maintain comprehensive plan	Maintain comprehensive plan
Athlete support services	Training Table (in season); pregame meal budget		Vision enhancement program	Player education program	

Collaboration

The very first thing I tell any assistant coach who works with me is that I expect my assistants to be collaborators in a mutual effort to produce team success, and not merely passive conduits of orders from the head coach. I expect my assistants to take an aggressive role in raising questions, advancing proposals, evaluating my motives for doing one thing instead of another—in short, serving as a partner in the ongoing task of setting the proper course for our program. This has been a central concept in my efforts to create winning teams.

There is a built-in risk in inviting assistants to become collaborators. Many coaches recognize this and prefer the safer, less stressful authoritarian mode, which allows the head coach to operate without being second-guessed. Under the authoritarian format, assistants are expected to stay in a holding pattern, waiting to carry out the next instruction from the head coach. The collaboration format is riskier. Every decision is questioned for its validity and relevance in advancing team goals. Each participant must possess a relatively healthy ego. Otherwise, hurt feelings and emotional sidetracking can produce flaring tempers and other unwanted distractions.

Here is an example of how this works. I used to have a problem with keeping my frustrations in check during matches. I'd let a referee's call or a player's mistake get to me, and I'd go off, veins bulging in my temples, staring hateful daggers at my victims, saying rude and unnecessary things to people with as much disgust and self-righteous anger as I could muster. Don Hardin used to tell me how uncharacteristic of me this behavior was and, because it negatively affected the motivational atmosphere of our players, how it acted as an obstacle in our attempt to achieve our goals. I understood this on an intellectual level. But I had a difficult time suppressing these unwanted demons when they took control of me during matches.

One night in 1984, we were playing at Bradley University. It was a long and frustrating match. We were winning, but we were playing terribly. I was convinced we were getting the short end of the stick from the officials. I launched into my madman act. And right in the middle of it, right when I was about to come up with my best stuff, Don walked up to me near the sideline and said, "Mike, this is bullshit. The team is out there trying to win a match, and you're more interested in proving to everyone how upset you are." I got mad. "I can coach," I shot back at him. "I've been around a lot longer than you have." I was defensive and couldn't believe he would say that to me.

But later on I had time to think the matter through. He was absolutely right, and he had the courage to tell me so at precisely the moment I needed to hear it. Not only that, he had done exactly what I had asked him to do. I had always told him not to hold anything back. And this meant *anything*. There are no executive privileges in a true collaboration. Everyone must be willing to listen and to evaluate, including the head coach. This inevitably leads to potentially explosive episodes, such as the one I've described. But a genuine commitment to the principle of collaboration is usually sufficient to provide the strength to work through the rough moments. Its rewards definitely outweigh its drawbacks.

Consistency

It is imperative that a staff present itself in a consistent fashion to its players. Differences of opinion may surface in staff meetings, but once the matter is settled, all staff members must stay in step when addressing the team. It is confusing and disruptive to players when coaches drag petty squabbles into the practice gym. This can only impede the team's pursuit of its goals.

Timing is also important. It is rarely productive when one coach interrupts another to criticize or disagree in front of the team. There is a delicate balance to be established. On the one hand, I believe in the principle of collaboration and constant evaluation of every component of the program. But on the other, the players need to be given clear direction and purpose. The staff can wage a heated, continuous debate over programmatic concepts, but when it is time to address the team, the staff must deliver a consistent, coherent message.

Maintaining staff consistency requires maturity and self-control among the coaches. While serving as my assistant, Don Hardin often felt that he had a better way to do something, whether it was running a certain drill or organizing our defensive system of play. But he often sensed it was not the right time to bring it up and deferred to the notion that staff consistency was more important—at least, for the moment. There were times when he knew I was wrong about something, but felt that the head coach had made a decision and it was better to go with it. Yet by picking the right time and place, he always found a way to get his views on the table. These are skills that are cultivated over time. It is the head coach's responsibility to set an example and create an atmosphere that promotes the principle of staff consistency.

Winning the Bureaucracy Battle

I don't think I'll ever meet a group of professionals who feel more persecuted than volleyball coaches. It comes from our perception that we are treated as second-class citizens in the world of athletics. We also carry a chip on our shoulders over the fact that so many people think volleyball is basically a recreational, sissy sport.

I like to loosen up audiences sometimes with this little bit. If I were the head football coach being introduced, I tell them, your eyes would be sparkling with anticipation. You would be envisioning fleet-footed wide receivers in full stride hauling in touchdown passes and running backs leaving tacklers strewn all over the field as they zigzag for the score. If I were the head basketball coach, you would smile, applaud, and feel the thunder of the slam jam executed by our all-American power forward. And if I were the track coach, tennis coach, golf coach—you get the idea—there would be an immediate association with the athletic drama of that coach's sport. But this doesn't hold true for volleyball. When I am introduced to general audiences, the only image that comes to mind is the volleyball game at the company picnic—the game with 20 or 30 people on each side of the net, a barrel of beer at courtside, and a net tied between two trees. I look out over the audience and see all these quizzical expressions peering back at me. Trust me, I tell them, come watch us play, and I guarantee you'll come back.

Volleyball and Basketball

We don't like having to fight this image problem all the time. And we also don't like having to fight the basketball war. There are many high school athletes who would like to specialize in volleyball by playing exclusively with a club team each year after their scholastic season is over. However, the volleyball club season conflicts with high school basketball, and many of the good volleyball players are also counted on to play on the basketball team. Basketball coaches don't handle this very well. They behave as though there exists in the universe a self-evident axiom that stipulates that where a choice exists between the two sports, an athlete should obviously choose basketball, which they believe to hold a superior position on the ladder of sport worthiness.

This same axiomatic principle seems to govern basketball coaches' philosophy of facility usage. They apparently believe that a gym is in its natural state when the floor is clear of everything but basketball hoops and basketball court lines. A volleyball net is seen as an intrusion, an abnormality that can be tolerated only after the last basketball player has thrown a final, postgame flip shot on the way to the locker room. Only a volleyball coach can know the utter disgust basketball coaches freely express when volleyball lines are taped or—and they consider this an atrocity of the highest order—painted on *their* basketball court. We have spent a lifetime stewing over the arrogance of our brothers and sisters who happen to coach a game that uses only 5 people and plays with a brown-colored ball, larger and heavier than a volleyball.

And this is not to mention the legions of recreational basketball players, who crowd impatiently around our courts as we wind up our practice sessions, seething with disgust that we are taking up valuable time from the hoops. I was once physically threatened by a guy who—and this is no joke—claimed that my varsity volleyball team was interfering with his constitutional and God-given right to play pickup basketball!

Task-Oriented Behavior

Yes, volleyball coaches grow up feeling indignant over the treatment their sport receives. This is why we have such a short fuse whenever we arrive at budget or facility meetings. We are emotional, ready to put our life on the line over seemingly insignificant matters. Considering the years of frustration each of us has endured, our self-righteousness seems understandable. But it has absolutely no place in our attempt to build our sport and our profession. In fact, it serves only to retard and nullify our efforts.

Like any group seeking to accomplish goals and having to rely on administrative bureaucracies to do so, we have to attempt to understand administrators' realities and develop a plan and a dialogue that can produce results. This means putting a lid on our boiling cauldron of emotions. It means becoming task-oriented and developing a style that is compatible with and supportive of the administrators and bureaucrats upon whom we rely for success.

In 1983, as I said earlier, Kenney Gym was a coach's nightmare. It was both our practice and competition facility, yet we had no control over it. The University of Illinois had essentially abandoned it, throwing it like a bone to the community as a place anyone on the street could walk in and use. I tried, on many occasions, to reserve it at night or on weekends for a supplemental setter workout and would be turned down. I would drive over to the gym to check out what was going on. I saw dozens of people playing hoops, no one checking to see if they were students or not. I saw teenagers on bicycles riding across the floor, unsupervised. I saw young kids drinking beer and smoking cigarettes in the balcony. The place was a zoo. No one cared, no one was around to monitor what went on in the building. All I knew was that I went through official channels and was turned down, yet all this other stuff was apparently OK.

Something had to change. I had been hired to build a championship program. But nobody was doing anything to provide an even minimally acceptable facility in which this championship team was supposed to train and compete. For a while I fumed, kicked, and screamed. I tried to shame administrators into rectifying this wrong. My volleyball program meant so much to me. Why couldn't they understand?

They did understand. But they wouldn't do anything about it, because I had created an atmosphere that prevented them from responding. After all, who is going to go out of the way to help someone who is holding a gun on them?

After a time, I realized that if I wanted results I had to behave in a different fashion. I had to present the issue in such a way that they would see that it would be in their own best interests to solve the problem. I had to begin thinking like an administrator, seeing the problem from that perspective. I argued that tightening up the scheduling procedures and re-examining the usage patterns of Kenney Gym would restore a sense of integrity to the building and return it to the mainstream of campus life. I pointed out that a building security plan would fit nicely with the university's ongoing concern for increased campus safety. And I explained that the improvements associated with our being in the building—floor renovation, locker room improvements, better lighting, new public-address system, new scoreboards, and so on—would benefit other users of the facility.

I began talking their language, and the results were immediate. I had given them some room to operate. In the process I made sure that I forged some friendships and treated everyone with the respect I would like extended to me. And I made sure I thanked them. I wanted them to feel good about having the chance to work with and for the volleyball program.

These people don't need to feel the sting of our frustrations. That only gets in the way. We need to be diplomatic and results-oriented. Every problem has a solution, and it is the head coach's job to survey the situation and the people involved to make sure the solution captures the interests and motives of all relevant parties. Defuse the emotional content, create a winning strategy, and finish it off by giving credit to the people who authorize the solution. This is how you win the bureaucracy battle.

Division of Labor

One of the most challenging experiences for any head coach is to create a division of labor to be implemented by the coaching staff. The challenge lies in sorting out and identifying the full range of tasks involved in running a program. We are sometimes overwhelmed by the number and diversity of issues that come at us every day. It is important to have a map of the various components of the program and a predetermined plan that indicates who is assigned to handle which task. I have included such a plan in the appendix to this chapter.

It is important to understand that my plan fits my particular circumstances. You may not have access to three assistants like I do. Or you may have additional task categories you deem critical to your program's success. Whatever your circumstances, the concept is the same. First, you have to itemize the tasks to be accomplished. And second, *you* have to assign, from the people available to you, the right person for each task.

Wrap-Up

There is a difference between building a team and building a program. A team can have one great season and fall out of contention in subsequent seasons. A program can achieve success over time. Programs have a yearly plan for recruiting and developing new talent, creating and maintaining good public relations, updating and refining coaching skills, funding all aspects of program operations, and monitoring the organization plan. This well-planned structure means that, year after year, programs are capable of fielding quality teams. Being a successful coach over time requires, therefore, that a coach develop not only the skills to teach Xs and Os, but also the skills to build a comprehensive program.

Appendix

Coaching Tasks

The following is a recent example of an itemization of tasks I wrote for use in the University of Illinois volleyball program. I do not include the actual staff assignments. They can be doled out in whatever manner the head coach sees fit.

University of Illinois Volleyball

I. Administration
    A. Develop and manage the program
        1. Develop program organization scheme
        2. Develop plan for staff division of labor
        3. Develop plan for staff training and evaluation
        4. Develop team competition goal structure for application to all program areas
    B. Develop a plan for staff protocol and ground rules
        1. Confidentiality
        2. Debate protocol (i.e., collaboration)

3. Formal communication mechanisms
   a. Memo habit
   b. Written proposals to express ideas
4. Office hours
5. Dress code
6. Office regulations and red tape (travel expense reports, etc.)
7. Yearly calendar coordination (outside clinics, appearances, etc.)
8. Compliance responsibilities (Big Ten and NCAA)
9. Office maintenance

C. Develop and manage the budget
   1. Develop annual program budget
   2. Monitor budget expenditures to ensure fiscal responsibility
      a. All expenses approved by Mike
      b. All travel advances and expense reports completed by individual coach, then signed by head coach
      c. All expenses reported to secretary for recording by line item

D. Regular staff meetings
   1. Have minutes typed and distributed by morning after each meeting
   2. Develop record-keeping system for staff agendas, minutes, etc.

E. Arrange team travel
   1. Develop team travel plan for fall and spring seasons
   2. Prepare trip-by-trip cost estimates for approval by head coach
   3. Secure all necessary transportation, lodging, and meal arrangements
   4. Prepare all necessary travel advances and expense reports
   5. Prepare rooming lists and itineraries for each trip

F. Coordinate the facility
   1. Develop a year-round facility schedule for practice and competition
   2. Communicate in timely fashion with facilities coordinators in order to secure needed space
   3. Manage team locker room and Kenney office/storage cage maintenance
      a. Plan for regular cleaning and maintenance
      b. Plan for aesthetic quality
      c. Plan for bulletin board maintenance (content, decisions, updates, etc.)

G. Coordinate player affairs
   1. Develop and distribute player manual

    2. Schedule and conduct regular player meetings

    3. Develop a plan for monitoring academic progress and eligibility

       a. Liaison with Academic Services Office

       b. Weekly reports to staff

H. Develop competition schedules for fall and spring seasons

I. Identify and order all necessary equipment

J. Supervise team managers

    1. Payroll paperwork

    2. Statistics assignments

    3. Videotape assignments

    4. Duty assignments (set-up, take-down, etc.)

    5. Travel schedule

K. Make miscellaneous staff assignments

    1. Officials' evaluations

    2. Liaisons

       a. Facilities

       b. Equipment

       c. Trainer

       d. Academic Services

       e. Sports Information

       f. Event Management

       g. Illini Pride

       h. Training Table

    3. Competition schedule and player and staff roster

       a. Develop

       b. Distribute

       c. Update

    4. Plan home pregame meal schedule

L. Arrange special projects

    1. Spring tournament (make facility reservations, solicit teams, coordinate with Networkers, etc.)

    2. Alumni match

    3. Banquet presentation

    4. Contract negotiations (shoes, balls, apparel, etc.)

    5. Team locker room

M. Conduct Fighting Illini Volleyball Camps

II. Technical and Tactical Structure

A. Develop a seasonal plan

    1. Analyze conference, regional, and national competition annually

    2. Establish peak competition goals for collegiate season

B. Guidelines for a system of play

C. A plan for training the team
  1. Develop a year-round training schedule
  2. Plan, write out, and keep a record for each practice
  3. Develop a system for filing practice plans
  4. Develop a training philosophy which includes
     a. Theoretical base for motor learning and skill acquisition (technique); key words for each skill
     b. Theoretical base for learning team tactics
     c. Plan for including competitive drills and games in the practice format, including incentive aware system
  5. Develop a plan for on-court team communication patterns, which include
     a. Identification of the situations calling for communication
     b. Development of a common language for players to use in these situations
     c. Systematic training for the on-court use of these communication patterns
  6. Develop a staff division of labor for practice, which includes assignments in areas such as
     a. Primary practice-planner and -recorder
     b. Warm-up and cool-down
     c. Setter training
     d. Blocking
     e. Passing and defensive ball control
     f. Serving
     g. Spiking technique
     h. System tactics—Offense
     i. System tactics—Defense
     j. Physical training
     k. Alternate training for injured players
  7. Develop and distribute practice policies and procedures
D. Evaluating practice and match performance
  1. Video program
     a. Prepare individual player tapes (edited compilations of practice/match footage); plan for systematic compilation
     b. Prepare a plan for recording and filing match tapes
     c. Prepare a system for utilizing tape at practice site
     d. Prepare a plan for systematic, regular viewing of individual and team tapes by players (with staff supervision)
  2. Statistics program
     a. Develop a system for recording and summarizing match statistics with attention to an efficient time frame for delivering statistical summaries to staff

      b. Decide what statistics should be kept and monitor their usefulness in improving the team's performance

      c. Develop a system for efficient retrieval of information on selected matches, players, and statistical categories

      d. Distribute statistical summary sheets to players for inclusion in player manuals

  E. Develop a plan for scouting and game planning

    1. Develop a plan for securing videotapes on selected opponents

    2. Develop a calendar for assigning necessary scouting trips

    3. Ensure that staff is in compliance with all NCAA and Big Ten rules related to scouting

    4. Prepare scouting reports on selected opponents

      a. Develop form to guide preparation

      b. Assign staff members to "specialize" on selected teams

      c. Develop a record-keeping system for all scouting reports (include all brochures, press releases, etc.)

    5. Prepare specific game plans for selected opponents

      a. Distribute plan to team

      b. Assign 1 staff member to prepare and coach a scout team against whom game plans can be practiced

  F. Develop a staff division of labor for match management

    1. Prematch preparation

      a. Pregame meeting agenda

      b. Pregame imagery session

      c. Warm-up supervision

    2. Match

      a. Collection of statistics

      b. Match analysis/adjustments; information flow

      c. Time-out supervision

      d. Personnel (lineup, substitutions)

      e. Agenda for midmatch meeting

    3. Postmatch

      a. Cool-down supervision and locker room protocol

      b. Postgame meeting agenda

      c. Statistical summary preparation and delivery to staff

  G. Assign special projects (staff assignments)

    1. Blocking or defending against the slide

    2. Selection of which statistics to use

    3. Use of video and computer to enhance practice and performance

III. Recruiting

  A. Develop a plan for maximizing compliance with NCAA and Big Ten rules

    1. Maintain an up-to-date file of current recruiting legislation

2. Develop a plan for educating staff and players on current legislation
3. Develop and maintain an accurate record-keeping system for use throughout the recruiting process
   a. Record official contacts (on and off campus, campus paid visits, etc.)
   b. Record all advances, expense, reports, use of host money, etc.
   c. Maintain records for required number of years (NCAA rule)

B. Develop a plan for identifying potential recruits
1. Develop and coordinate a system for responding to all written inquiries
   a. Develop a filing system
   b. View and return videotapes in a timely fashion (copy, if warranted)
2. Develop and coordinate a year-round plan for on-site talent evaluation
3. Develop and update a system for identifying those athletes we should recruit (by class and by priority)
4. Serve as liaison with Academic Services in evaluating a potential recruit's academic eligibility

C. Develop strategies for recruiting these student athletes to the University of Illinois
1. Develop a system for communicating with recruits
   a. Develop and maintain an inventory of letters for mailing to recruits
   b. Develop and monitor a plan for systematic mail contact with each recruit
   c. Develop and monitor a plan for systematic telephone contact with each recruit
2. Develop a system for utilizing the allowable contacts with each recruit
   a. Develop and coordinate a schedule of home or campus visits for each recruit
   b. Develop and distribute to the staff a content outline for material to be covered during home and campus visits
   c. Develop and coordinate a schedule of campus paid and unpaid visits
      (1) Select hosts
      (2) Develop and distribute itineraries
      (3) Prepare team for maximum visit effectiveness
      (4) Function as on-campus coordinator for each visit

     D. Develop a staff protocol for ranking and signing recruits, including
       1. Procedures for deciding who offers each scholarship, when it is to be offered, and to whom it is offered
       2. Procedures for signing recruits to scholarships
     E. Accept responsibility for initiating within staff all recruiting-related proposals, updates, assignments, and other matters
     F. Develop a system for evaluating the effectiveness of each component of our recruiting strategy

IV. Player Development
     A. Develop and implement a year-round physical training program, which includes
       1. Strength training
       2. Cardiovascular conditioning
       3. Flexibility training
     B. Develop and maintain a system for testing and recording physical testing data
     C. Develop and conduct a year-round player education program that includes items such as
       1. Lifestyle management
       2. Communication skills
         a. Interpersonal relations
         b. Problem-solving strategies
         c. Feedback-giving skills
       3. Sport psychology skills
       4. Statistical evaluation
       5. Media and other personal appearances
       6. Compliance with NCAA regulations
       7. Opponent education
         a. Reports on selected teams
         b. Scouting techniques
       8. Playing rules
     D. Develop and administer player surveys and questionnaires
       1. Preseason
       2. Midseason
       3. Postseason
     E. Develop and distribute player manual
       1. System of play
       2. Schedule
       3. Protocol, team rules, procedures
       4. Travel itineraries
       5. Compliance handouts
       6. Miscellaneous information

V. Public Relations
    A. Develop a public relations program for the U of I volleyball pro-
        gram, including frequent and personal contact with both indi-
        viduals and corporate supporters
    B. Assign and schedule all public-speaking requests and appear-
        ances of staff
    C. Write and distribute the monthly "Side-out Newsletter"
        1. Create and update the mailing list (include parents, Net-
            workers, etc.)
        2. Arrange for monthly mailing
    D. Serve as liaison between volleyball program and Networkers
        1. Attend all booster meetings
        2. Send appropriate thank-you letters
        3. Coordinate annual banquet activities
            a. Prepare a special-guest list
            b. Prepare a team or season presentation
            c. Obtain awards
            d. Transport awards, banners, etc. to and from the banquet

Game Planning
and Coaching

I have heard it said many times that a coach's job ends when the first whistle blows and the match begins. This line of reasoning seems to hold that if you prepare your team properly, you need only to relax on the bench and watch the match unfold. There isn't much you can do at this point. A coach would be well advised to sit back, take notes during the match, and plan the next practice session.

Like everyone else, I believe in thorough preparation. But I also believe that a coach can play a significant and sometimes decisive role in the outcome of a match. A calming influence here, a blocking adjustment there, a key substitution, a clear and confident directive in the face of adversity, or a show of faith at a critical moment—a coach can offer all these things and more. And their cumulative effect can spell the difference between winning and losing.

DEVELOPING THE GAME PLAN

In its simpler days, volleyball was played without the benefit of a game plan. Everyone played the same offensive and defensive styles that had been handed down from one generation of players to the next. There was very little time wasted on considering what the opponent might be doing on the other side of the net. We had not matured as a sport, and it showed. Sometimes it seemed that all the coach could come up with were things like, Watch out for the big dude; he hits the crap out of the ball.

Little by little, we became more sophisticated in our understanding of the game. Game planning began to appear on the scene. One of my early attempts to construct a game plan sticks in my mind as a reflection of how unique such efforts were once considered. I was coaching the men's team at the University of Pittsburgh. We were gathered in our pregame meeting, ready to take the floor against Penn State. There was a small blackboard on the locker room wall, and I decided to use it to review some key points. One by one, I listed the items on my list. They were simple things like matching up our best blocker against their top hitter, serving at weak receivers in certain rotations, and tipping the ball to undefended areas of the Penn State defense. But the fact that they were presented in a point-by-point, organized form was a new experience for most of the players. On the way out of the locker room, they talked about how much more focused they would be during the match. They walked a little taller knowing that their sport possessed the tactical sophistication that required the formulation of an actual *game plan*.

I saw that same look on the faces of my Nigerian students when I was in the Peace Corps. I worked among the Igbos, one of the many tribal groupings near the Niger River delta. As part of my Peace Corps training, I learned a little of the Igbo language. Igbo children learned their language only by hearing it spoken. But in the 1950s and '60s, some American linguists had studied Igbo and constructed a set of grammatical rules so it could be taught to nonnative speakers like me. When I showed the grammar workbook to my Nigerian students, they were astonished. The language they had spoken all their lives had a grammar, just like English, French, and German. They became instantly prouder and taller. They felt suddenly legitimate in the international linguistic community. And this, on an admittedly lesser scale, was how my volleyball players felt when they first learned that their sport could utilize game plans.

Gathering Information on Your Team

Constructing a game plan requires that a great deal of information be collected and interpreted. I recommend starting by gathering statistics on the three basic, individual performance categories: attacking, passing, and serving.

Attacking

Measuring the attack phase of the game requires that certain numbers be recorded. First, count each player's total attack attempts (TA). Then record that player's total number of kills (K) and errors (E). A kill is an attack that results directly in a point or side-out (i.e., hits the floor, or caroms off a defender out-of-play). An error is a ball that is attacked into the net or out-of-bounds, or is stuff-blocked by the opponent. All attacks that are not kills or errors are presumed to have been successfully defended and kept in play by the opponent. Thus it is possible to have more attack attempts than the sum of a player's kills and errors.

Two important statistics can be derived from this data. The first is the player's kill percentage. A kill percentage is calculated by dividing total kills by total attack attempts (K/TA). A player who registers 10 kills out of 20 attempts, for example, would score a .500 kill percentage. The second is the player's kill efficiency. Kill efficiency is calculated by subtracting errors from kills before dividing by total attempts ([K−E]/TA). This same player, by committing five errors, would post an attack efficiency of .250 (i.e., [10−5]/20). Kill percentage measures the frequency of a player's "put-away" potential. Kill efficiency measures the player's net effectiveness in the offensive scheme.

Passing

Passing accuracy can be measured in a variety of ways. The most commonly used format grades each pass on a sliding scale of 3 to 0, with 3 being a perfect pass and 0 representing a passing error. Two aspects of each pass are evaluated. First is the location. Generally speaking, if a pass is accurate enough to allow the setter to set all options in the offense, it is given a 3. A pass that pulls the setter far enough away from the offense origination point that the quick option in the offense cannot be set is given a 2. A pass that is significantly off target is graded as 1. Any time a player is aced or is called by the referee for a ball-handling violation, a 0 is recorded on that passing attempt.

Passes are also evaluated for their trajectory. The pass must be high enough and soft enough to enable the setter to establish position under the ball. But passes can be too high. A ball descending from too high a trajectory can be difficult to set, and the timing of the attack sequence can be disrupted. Passes can also be too low and too fast, thereby preventing the setter from having the time to manipulate the ball according to the offensive game plan. Therefore, a pass can be a 3 by location, but if it is too high or too low, it will be downgraded to a 2 or 1 depending on how far it deviates from the desired trajectory.

Each passing attempt by a player is given a score of 3, 2, 1, or 0. At the end of each game or match, a player's passing average can be calculated by dividing the total points accumulated by the total number of passing attempts. In Game 1, for example, a player may have passed 10 balls for scores of 3, 3, 0, 2, 1, 2, 3, 1, 2, and 3 (for a total of 20 points). This player's passing average for Game 1 would be 2.00 (20 points divided by 10 passes).

Serving

Serving is evaluated according to the same system used to grade passing, except in reverse. If a player serves a ball that results in a 3 pass by the opponent, the serve is awarded a 1. A 2 pass results from a 2 serve, and a 1 pass from a 3 serve. A serving error is given a 0. If a player serves an ace, I like to assign a score of 5, and I give a 4 to the player whose serve forces the opponent to pass the ball on the first contact back over to our side of the net (overpass). Serving scores look like this:

Pass	Serve	
ace	5	
overpass	4	
1	3	
2	2	
3	1	
—	0	(service error)

For example, a player might accumulate the following serving numbers in a match: 5, 5, 2, 0, 2, 1, 1, 4, 0, 2, 2, 1, 1, 2, and 2. This player's serve average for the match would be 2.00 (30 points divided by 15 serve attempts).

A coach can also use statistical analysis to evaluate and regulate the degree to which a team should serve aggressively or cautiously. The service ace is the easiest way to score a point. It results from only one contact of the ball. I believe a coach should decide roughly how many points a game his or her team should try to score as a result of service aces. A conservative approach might dictate that the team should serve cautiously and rely on other phases of the game, such as hitting, blocking and defense, to score points. Conservative serving coaches often feel that their team should never deprive itself of the opportunity to score a point by committing a service error. If aces come, so be it. But serving aces will not be the focus of the team's point-scoring philosophy.

A more aggressive approach might dictate that a team try to score, say, 3 or 4 points a game by way of the service ace. This would require an extremely aggressive serving philosophy. Everyone on the team would have to be given "the green light to go for it" from the service line.

Because going for the ace almost always requires a more aggressive swing at the ball, the possibility for committing serving errors increases. The coach must decide just how many errors will be tolerated in the effort to score aces. In statistical terms, the coach must decide on an acceptable ace-to-error ratio. If a player serves 6 aces in a match and commits only 3 errors, the ace-to-error ratio would be 2:1. Most coaches would be delighted with these numbers. But what if those 6 aces were accompanied by 12 errors for a 1:2 ratio? Many coaches would say that the aces were achieved at too high a cost. Six points were scored, but that same server gave up 12 opportunities to score by other means.

For me, given the realities of the NCAA Division I women's collegiate game, I have settled on trying to score at least 2.5 points a game via the ace. And I can live with an ace-to-error ratio of 1:1.2. These figures are the result of my own predispositions about the role of serving in the overall point-scoring effort, and of a long-term analysis of serving statistics and their correlation to winning volleyball matches. For another coach at another level of play these numbers might be entirely different. This is for you to decide.

I keep one last serving statistic that I think can be helpful in regulating the service game. All players should be evaluated in terms of the percentage of aces and errors each serves. This figure can be calculated by dividing total aces by total serve attempts, and then dividing total errors by total attempts. I have decided over the years that I like my servers to record aces about 10% of the time. If I want my servers to achieve at least a 1:1.2 ace-to-error ratio, then I would expect that each server, in the effort to serve aces at least 10% of the time, would commit errors no more than 12% of the time. If in reviewing individual player statistics I find, for example, that a player is serving at only a 3% ace clip and is committing errors at only a 5% rate, I tell that player to turn up the heat on the serve. Here is a player who is serving too cautiously. I am willing to risk more errors (up to 12% total) to see if I can squeeze more aces (hopefully 10%) out of this player's serving game. But if another player is at 3% aces and 17% errors, I have a much different problem. Here is a player who probably has poor serving technique and needs fundamental training. The last thing in the world I want to tell this player is to serve tougher. The error percentage would likely go through the roof and make serving tougher a poor risk, no matter how close to the 10% ace standard that player might come.

 All of these serving statistics are important: serve average, aces per game, ace-to-error ratio, and ace and error percentages. A coach must weigh each independently and then together in order to fine tune a serving strategy for a given team.

Team Statistics

Each of these individual statistics—attack, pass, and serve—can be kept on a team basis as well. It is important to have team totals in every category. Certain embellishments can be useful, too. In taking attack statistics, for example, you can separate attempts based on in- versus out-of-system passes. If you discover that your team attack efficiency is .344 when a 3 is passed, but only .109 when a 1 or 2 is passed, then you know you need some work on your out-of-system offense. You can also arrange your statistics worksheet so that you record attack attempts according to the type of set delivered (e.g., high outside, quick, second tempo, and so on) This enables you to keep tabs on how effectively each phase of the offensive game is operating.

And finally, it can be extremely helpful to record passing statistics by rotation. This requires that a coach first have a shorthand way of naming each rotation. I solve this by identifying the rotation according to the position of the setter in my 5-1 alignment. If the setter is in Position 1, then we are in Rotation 1. The next rotation would be Rotation 6, because the setter would have rotated one position to the left (i.e., Position 6). In my scheme of things, the rotations are numbered, in order, 1, 6, 5, 4, 3, and 2. When a pass is executed while our setter is in Position 4, the passer's score goes under "Rotation 4" (see Figure 7.1). At the end of the game or match, I calculate our team's passing average in each rotation. This enables me to spot the weak passing rotations and gives me valuable direction in designing ways to strengthen our passing technique.

Point Chart

There are only four ways to terminate play in volleyball: aces, kills, stuff blocks, or errors. It is important to keep a record of how your team scores and gives up points. This information provides a personality sketch of your team and is one more important clue in determining just what areas of the team's performance might need the most work.

Either you or someone you assign should record the disposition of each point for or against your team. This can be done using a worksheet or handheld tape recorder or by reviewing videotape after the match. A manager records our data using a worksheet and clipboard, scoring a notation under either "Illinois" or "Opponent" for each point. Table 7.1 shows a hypothetical worksheet.

Illinois won this hypothetical game 15-12. The notations would have been summarized as shown in Table 7.2.

If I were to analyze this game on the basis of the point chart, I would be pleased that my team had *earned* 12 of its 15 points. Only 3 were handed to us by unforced opponent errors. This means we were playing well. I would especially like the fact that we served, blocked, and defended well enough to score 7 points with transition counterattacking. But on the other hand, we let our opponent score too easily. They

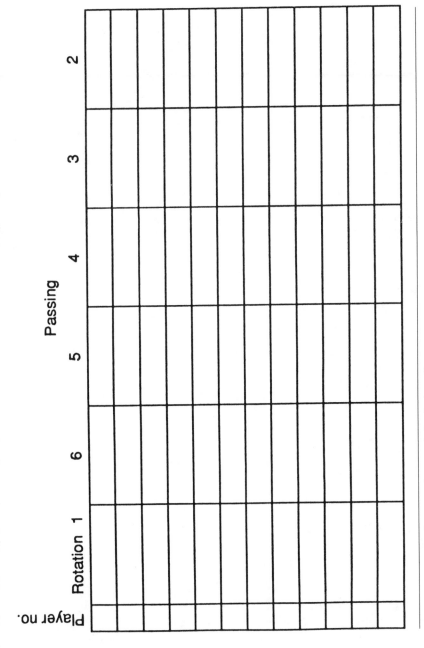

Figure 7.1 Recording passing statistics by rotation.

Table 7.1 Point Chart

Illinois		Point number	Opponent	
Type of play	Player		Type of play	Player
Kill by Ill #9		1	Ace by Opp #2	
BHE by Opp #11		2	AE by Ill #14	
NVE by Opp #5		3	Ace by Opp #6	
Kill by Ill #12		4	BHE by Ill #12	
Ace by Ill #5		5	AE by Ill #15	
SB by Ill #5/15		6	AE by Ill #9	
Kill by Ill #15		7	NVE by Ill #12	
Kill by Ill #12		8	Kill by Opp #7	
SB by Ill #4/12	9		AE by Ill #4	
AE by Opp #10		10	SB by Opp #9	
Ace by Ill #15		11	BHE by Ill #12	
Kill by Ill #12		12	Ace by Opp #7	
SB by Ill #7/15		13		
Kill by Ill #15		14		
Kill by Ill #15		15		

Note. B = stuff block; BHE = ball handling error; NVE = net violation error; AE = attack error.

Table 7.2 Summary of Point Chart

Points for		Points against	
Kind	Number	Kind	Number
Opp error	3	Ill error	7
Ace	2	Ace	3
Stuff block	3	Stuff block	1
Kill	7	Kill	1
Total	15		12

"earned" only 5 of their 12 points (three aces, one stuff block, and one kill). We committed seven unforced errors for points against us. So though we scored points efficiently, we gave them up carelessly through hitting errors, ball-handling errors, and a net violation.

By keeping this chart over a series of matches, you can get a solid feel for how your team is scoring its points. Are you earning them by playing sound volleyball? Or are you winning games because of the ineptness of your opponents, meaning you need to be on the lookout for a false sense of security developing among your players? Knowing the point chart can help you determine your approach to monitoring and regulating the competitive outlook of your team.

You can also identify tendencies in how opponents are scoring against you. Focus on the categories where you are losing the most points and work to fortify your defense. If, for example, you are being aced frequently, then your team obviously needs to improve its passing. Or if you're being stuff-blocked for points more than two or three times a game, you need to teach your hitters to attack around or in the seam of the block. It is also useful to record point-scoring data by rotation. Accumulating data over several matches reveals not only which area of the game is costing your team the most points, but also which rotations seem to be the primary culprits.

Net Points Won and Lost by Rotation

One of the first statistics I review to diagnose our team is a box on my statistical summary form entitled "Net Score By Rotation" (see Figure 7.2). This box tells me which rotations are healthy and which are not in terms of scoring and giving up points. The data for this box can be taken directly from the official scoresheet after the match. Don't ever leave a match without a copy of the scoresheet—it contains a great deal of valuable information!

Each circle (in Figure 7.2) is divided into six wedges, each wedge representing a different rotation. Each circle is also divided into an inner and an outer circle. The numbers of points won or lost in each rotation are recorded in a specific wedge. Illinois points are recorded in the outer circle, and opponent points in the inner circle. Imagine that the net is at the top of the circle. The right-back wedge is Rotation 1, the middle-back wedge is Rotation 6, the left-back wedge is Rotation 5, and so on. From the scoresheet I can determine how many points my team scored in, for example, Rotation 4. I can locate this information on the scoresheet by identifying who was serving when my setter was in the left-front position (Position 4). I count the number of points scored by that server and enter that number in the outer circle of the Rotation 4 wedge. I then count up the number of points scored by our opponent while we were in Rotation 4 and enter that number in the inner circle of the Rotation 4 wedge. By subtracting the opponent's total points from our total points, I come up with Illinois's net score for Rotation 4.

This same calculation is made for each rotation and for each game. The net scores for each rotation are then recorded in the spaces below each circle. The game totals are then summarized into a match total. This provides the coach with the net scoring totals by rotation for the match.

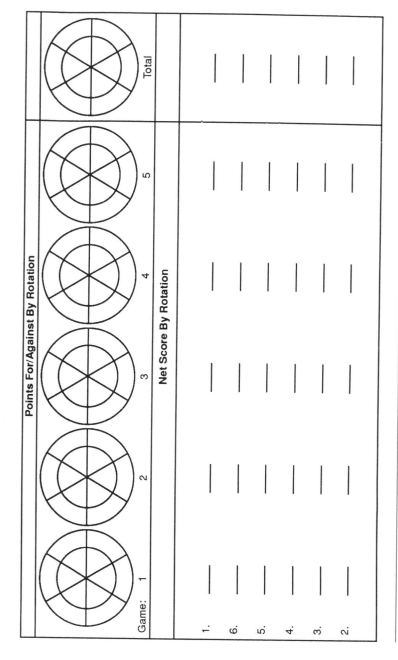

Figure 7.2 "Net Score By Rotation" form.

Let's take a look at a hypothetical five-game match and how these statistics are recorded (see Figure 7.3).

Despite being outscored 62-60, Illinois won this very close match. A glance at the rotational net scoring reveals a great deal about how this match was played. The most glaring piece of evidence is that we suffered a net loss of 14 points in Rotation 1. I do not consider it significant if the net totals—plus or minus—do not add up to more than the total number of games played. In this case, a net score of plus or minus 5 (or less) is not significant. The net scores in Rotations 5 (+4), 4 (0), and 3 (+4), therefore, do not concern me one way or the other. We played our opponent to a standoff in these rotations. Rotation 6 (−7) is noteworthy, but close to the integer 5 that would be used as a cutoff standard for this five-game match and therefore only a borderline problem. And Rotation 2 (+11) was an obvious delight to behold. We outscored our opponent by an average of over 2 points a game in this rotation. But Rotation 1 (−14) is a real problem. This means that we suffered a net loss of almost 3 points a game in Rotation 1. This was a sick rotation for us, and the coach's job is to find out why.

The first task is to ascertain just what kind of problem exists. A look at the total points scored (4) versus total points surrendered (18) in Rotation 1 gives us the first clue. These numbers tell me that we have a dual problem. First of all, we had difficulty scoring points. Four was the lowest scoring total of any rotation. This means that the point-scoring mechanisms of the game—serving, blocking, and counterattacking—were not functioning well for us in Rotation 1. But we also gave up 18 points, more than in any other rotation. This means that the point prevention mechanisms—passing and serve-receive offense—were not functioning well either. These insights mean a further search into the statistics is needed to find out what went wrong in Rotation 1. I can look at the individual passing, hitting, and serving stats, the error charts, and whatever else we've recorded, and sooner or later I can track down the source of the problem. This is the value of keeping the rotational net points chart. It gives you immediate feedback as to which rotations are costing the team points and so require closer study.

I'd like to add a word of clarification. The example in Figure 7.3 depicted Rotation 1 as having both point-scoring and point-yielding deficiencies. This is not always the case. Suppose the −14 net score had been the result of scoring 10 points in Rotation 1 but giving up 24 points. The 10 points on the scoring side would mean it was an adequate scoring rotation relative to the other rotations (16, 11, 5, 15, and 9). The problem would not be an inability to score points. But the giving-up of 24 points would put it way out of line with the other rotations, in terms of points scored against (5, 7, 5, 11, and 16). This would indicate that the villain in Rotation 1 would have been the inability to keep the *opponent* from

Points For/Against By Rotation

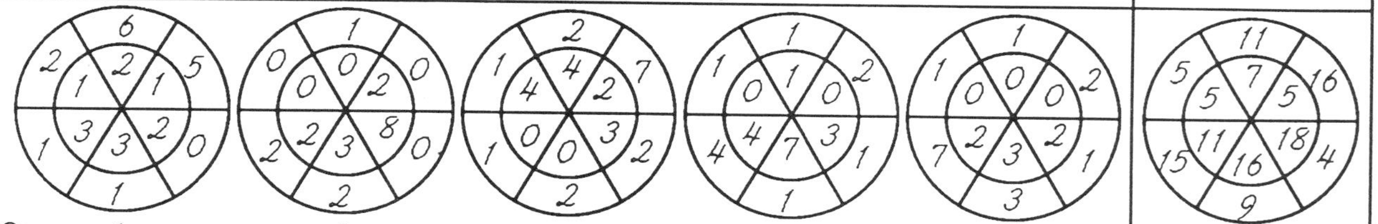

Game:	1	2	3	4	5	Total

Net Score By Rotation

	1	2	3	4	5	Total
1.	−2	−8	−1	−2	−1	−14
6.	−2	−1	+2	−6	0	−7
5.	−2	0	+1	0	+5	+4
4.	+1	0	−3	+1	+1	0
3.	+4	+1	−2	0	+1	+4
2.	+4	−2	+5	+2	+2	+11

Figure 7.3 Statistics recorded in "Net Score By Rotation" form.

scoring, and that this is where the coach should focus some corrective efforts. Knowing the actual breakdown of points for and against, in addition to the final net scores, is important in properly diagnosing a team's rotational health.

Gathering Information on Your Opponent

A comprehensive knowledge of your opponent begins with the same statistical data on them that you have on your own team. It is important to know each player's hitting percentages, who gets the most sets, who passes well or poorly, who serves well and who doesn't, and how this particular team tends to score and give up points. Knowing which rotations are strong or weak in terms of points won and lost can provide valuable insight on which players to match up or how to attack in a particular situation. Obtaining this information means that someone must record statistics, either in person, at a series of matches involving that opponent, or by reviewing videotapes of them.

Attack Tendencies

Of equal importance is the gathering of tactical information on the opponent's system of play. One of the most helpful tools in deciphering attacking style is the Side-out Offense Chart (see Figure 7.4). The information recorded on this chart gives you a summary picture of the set distribution and attack patterns in each rotation for the opponent's first ball side-out offense.

The recorder should watch from behind the baseline of the team being scouted, in order to get an unobstructed view of its serve-receive and approach patterns. The rotational order is recorded in the rotation wheel (see Figure 7.4) in the far left column. The court diagrams to the right of the wheel are used to diagram the serve reception patterns deployed in each successive rotation. Most teams use the same pattern throughout a match, but some like to change their receiving formations from time to time. The extra court diagrams can be used to draw any alternative formations.

The recorder next sketches the actual attack patterns of each rotation. In Rotation 1, using the sample data in Figure 7.4, the left-side hitter (#9) approached only to hit a 5 set. The middle hitter (#4) showed a 3, 1, and slide 6, and the right-side hitter (#11) went for both a 9 and a 2. In Rotation 4, the quick hitter (#12) not only hit all the quick options, but she occasionally stayed outside to hit a 5 as well. The outside hitter (#5) would swing left or right to hit either a 5 or 9. A back row player (#9)

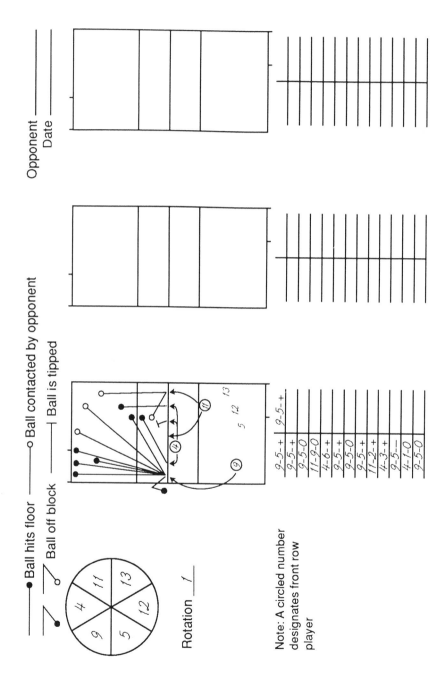

Opponent _____

Date _____

Ball hits floor ————●
Ball off block ——/
Ball contacted by opponent ————○
Ball is tipped ——|

Rotation __1__

Note: A circled number designates front row player

9-5-+
9-5-+
9-5-0
11-9-0
4-6-+
9-5-+
9-5-0
11-2-+
4-3-+
9-5--
4-1-0
9-5-0

176

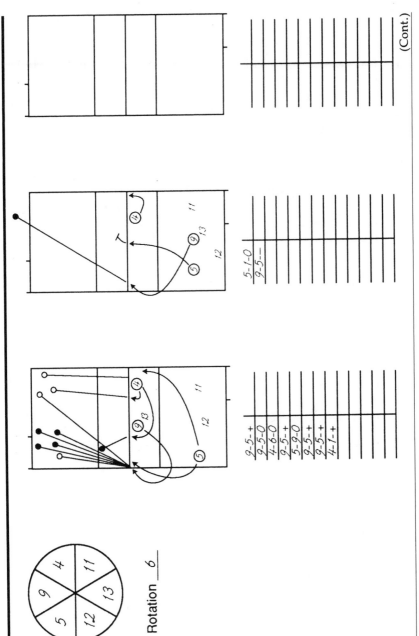

Figure 7.4 Side-out offense chart.

(Cont.)

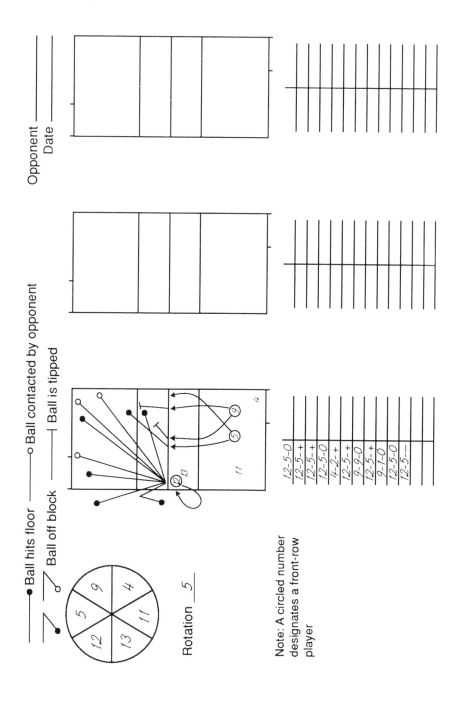

Opponent ——————
Date ——————

● Ball hits floor ———————— ○ Ball contacted by opponent

↗ ○ Ball off block ——| Ball is tipped

Rotation __5__

12	5	9
13	11	4

12-5-0
12-5-+
12-5-+
12-5-0
4-2-+
12-5-+
9-9-0
12-5-+
9-1-0
12-5-0
12-5--

Note: A circled number designates a front-row player

178

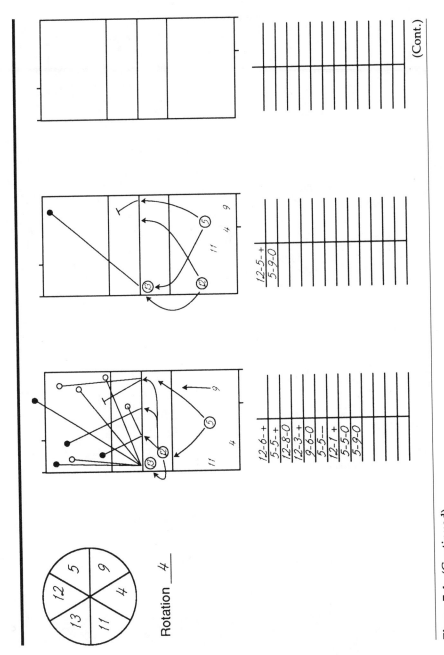

Rotation __4__

12-5- +
5-9-0

12-6- +
5-5- +
12-8-0
12-3- +
9-6-0
5-5- --
12-1- +
5-5-0
5-9-0

(Cont.)

Figure 7.4 (Continued)

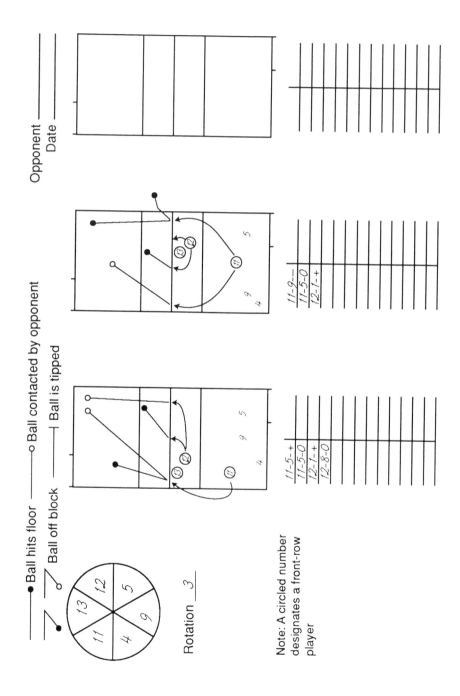

Opponent _____

Date _____

● Ball hits floor ——— ○ Ball contacted by opponent

⊣ Ball is tipped

Ball off block

Rotation _3_

13	12
11	5
4	9

11-5- +
11-5-0
12-1- +
12-8-0

11-9- —
11-5-0
12-1- +

Note: A circled number designates a front-row player

180

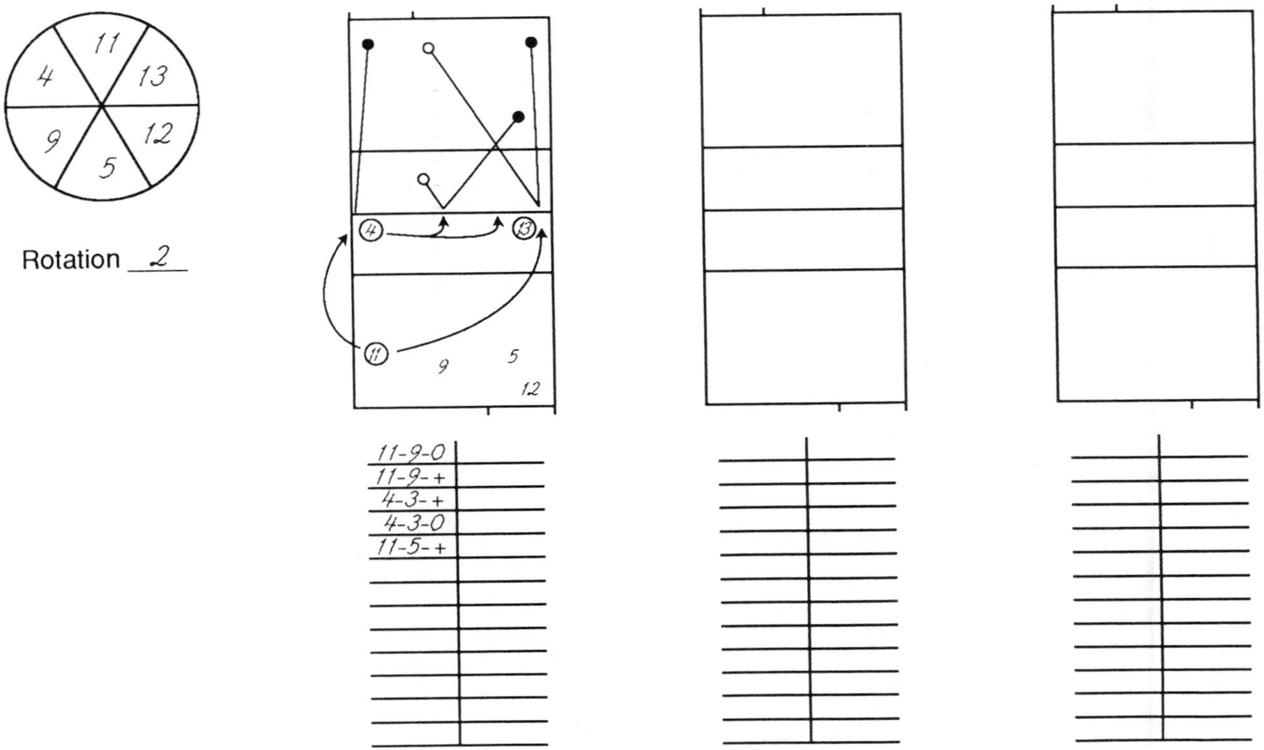

4
11
13
9
5
12
Rotation 2
4
13
11
9
5
12
11-9-0
11-9-+
4-3-+
4-3-0
11-5-+

Figure 7.4 (Continued)

was deployed to take a swing at a C set. Attack patterns, like these, must be charted for each receiving formation in each rotation.

The next step is to diagram the angle and location of each shot. For each attack, the recorder draws a line from the point of attack at the net to the point where the shot hits the floor or contacts an opponent (see examples in Figure 7.4). This data reveals the shot tendencies of individual hitters. Player #9 (in Rotations 1 and 6) tends to hit the ball consistently to the seam between Areas 1 and 6. If I were to set up a defense against this player, I would assign one of my deep defenders to move into that seam every time #9 gets a 5 set. The better hitters can attack all the angles and are more difficult to defend against. But if there are hitters who have tendencies that can be successfully countered, this chart will provide you that information.

Finally, I like to record the disposition of each attack. I use a 3-symbol code that tells me everything I need to know. The first entry in the code is the attacker's jersey number. The second identifies the set the attacker received. And the third indicates whether the attack was successful (+ is a kill; – is an error; o means that the attack was kept in play). I record this information in the columns below the court diagrams on the Side-out Chart. The first entry in Rotation 1 (see Figure 7.4) is 9-5-+. This means that Player #4 received a 1 set and got a kill.

Once I have compiled this information over the course of an entire match (or, preferably, over several matches), I examine the data to see if there are detectable tendencies in the opponent's side-out offense. Notice, for example, that in Rotation 5, Player #12 received a 5 set in 8 out of 11 serve-receive opportunities. Player #9 received 3 sets, and #5 was not set at all. This tells me that I can release my middle blocker to double-team against #12 and not have to worry too much about guarding against the quick set to #5. Most teams show similar tendencies in at least one or two rotations. Detecting them can give you a head start in designing a defensive game plan.

Defensive Tendencies

Tactical information on the opponent's defense can be just as useful. Prepare scouting worksheets so that the data listed in the box on the following page can be recorded.

Serving Tendencies

It is also important to know your opponent's serving tendencies. Do they serve accurately to particular zones, or do they just try to hit the ball hard regardless of location? Can they serve the short zones with

---

Data to Include on Defensive Scouting Worksheets

1. What blocking system are they using? Is the block bunched together or spread out in base position? Do they commit-block, or are they strictly a read-blocking team? Do they employ any special tactics, such as release- or stack-blocking? Do they ever switch blockers in an attempt to match up?
2. Gather information on individual blockers. Are the middle blockers slow or quick? Are they small or big? Do they reach into the angle well? Do the end blockers reach out to the line and invite the wipeoff shot? How do they react to second tempo sets? Are there any blockers so weak that we should direct our attack toward that blocker?
3. What defensive system are they using? Do they tend to block line or crosscourt? Do they defend the corners with a rotation-style defense, or do they defend with a perimeter-style? Do they move a player up to cover the tip? Do they change defenses during the match? Are there any special features about their defensive style that should be noted?

(This data should be charted for each rotation.)

control? Do they have players who can hit a good jump or topspin serve? Do they have serving substitutes? How good are they? Do they tend to serve from near the baseline, or do they serve from an area deep behind the baseline? Just as hitters in baseball can benefit from knowing the capabilities of opposing pitchers, receivers in volleyball can gain an edge by knowing the capabilities of each server.

Knowledge of Personnel

I also like to learn as much as possible about the psychology of my opponent. I watch teams to see which athletes play the role of stud, winner, or stabilizer, and which athletes do not contribute to this chemistry. I evaluate each player on the giver-versus-taker spectrum. I note whether players handle adversity well or poorly, and who plays well under pressure late in the match. I also like to know who the high-error players are.

I learn as much as I can about the opposing coach. What time-out and substitution patterns does this coach use? How does this coach respond to pressure, and what effect does he or she have on the psychological outlook of the team? If there is anger, is it controlled or not? What about this coach's ability to focus on the relevant events that make up the ebb and flow of a volleyball match? And what role does this coach play in the team's ability to gain or lose focus? Is this coach a help or a hindrance to the team?

The greatest benefit of having all this information on hand is the sense of confidence it gives me as I design a game plan and prepare to coach against a particular opponent. This confidence comes from knowing not only what my opponent is capable of technically and tactically, but also how they will most likely behave and respond. This alone would be sufficient reason to keep notes on opposing teams. But occasionally an extra benefit reveals itself: Sometimes, simply by knowing your opponent *psychologically,* you can help your team win the match.

I can recall many instances in my coaching career when this sort of information has been useful, but one episode stands out from all the rest. We were in a postseason tournament, play-off match. My team was a slight favorite against a quality opponent. We were playing well but found ourselves down 2-0 and heading into Game 3 with our backs to the wall. I had studied the opponent's head coach over the years and knew him to be volatile and likely to lose control of his emotions. Things had been going quite well for his team in the match, and he was feeling good and in control—making all the right decisions. But I sensed that if we could make one big push in the third game, if we could do something to threaten his team's apparent control of the match, we would trigger the "fear of losing" response in this coach, and he would start to unravel emotionally.

And that is exactly what I told my team. I knew my players were giving everything they had. If I had told them they had to give more, they would have been demoralized. You don't have to be superhuman over the span of three more games, I said. All you have to do is make a statement right now. If you can throw a scare into them in Game 3, their coach will blow his cool and that will take them out of the match. After that, you'll just have to hold on for the win.

The players bought into it. We turned up the heat and forced the opposing coach to call two early time-outs. I watched their huddle during each time-out and could see the steam start to rise. By the end of the game, he was yelling at his players after each error, gesturing with disgust. We won Game 3 easily. We also won Game 4. And when the teams took the baseline for the start of Game 5, some of his players were in tears, so humiliating had been his tirade during the 5-minute break. It was over before it started. We won the fifth game 15-3.

I'm not sure how I would have handled things during that match had I not studied the psychological patterns of the head coach. The other team had been playing so well, I don't know if I could have made a difference. I do know, however, that I felt very confident in what I had to say before Game 3. My brief speech was a turning point, one of the primary reasons we came back to win the match. And I also know that I would not have been ready with that speech had I not taken the time to learn all I could about the psychology of my opponent.

Designing the Game Plan

All of the information you gather on an opponent must be recorded in an organized fashion. This, in summary form, becomes the scouting report. But a scouting report is not a game plan. Game plans rely on the information in scouting reports, but are themselves selective interpretations of that information. No athlete or team can digest and apply all of the information contained in a thorough scouting report. It is the coach's job to decide which items are most important, to organize them into a specific game plan, and to present that plan to the players in a form they can easily understand.

Translate Scouting Information Into Directives

First, the coach must translate recorded data into directives. I have seen coaches hand out a rotational analysis and proceed to explain, point by point, what the opponent likes to do. "In Rotation 2," the coach might say, "their quick hitter likes to fake a 1 set and run behind the setter for a wide slide." This is important information, of course, and a coach might stop there, allowing the athletes to interpret it on their own. But that coach's job is only half done. What exactly would you want your players to do about defending against that wide slide? Telling your team what you want them to do—this must be the focus of the game plan. Recorded data is a necessary ingredient in preparing a game plan, but it plays only a supporting role. The central character is the game plan directive.

Here are some examples of directives derived from information typically contained in the scouting report:

Data: The opponent utilizes a three-person serve reception pattern. Their 3 outside hitters are their 3 receivers in every rotation.

Directive: In every rotation, we will serve deep to a front row receiver, in order to disrupt that hitter's ability to get into her attack pattern.

Data: The opponent's middle blockers are both tall and slow. They block well vertically but do not move well laterally.

Directive: Our in-system offense against this team will emphasize spreading the potential points of attack, in order to stress their middles with lateral movement. When attacking quick, we will use 3s and slides (not 1s). We will emphasize the 5-3-9 spread combination when in the three-hitter rotations, and the 5-slide and 3-8 or 3-9 combinations in the two-hitter rotations. We will avoid running quick and combination attacks into the middle of the net, where their tall blockers are camped out.

Data: Their offense is not discriminating in terms of pass and setter location. They do not rely on pinpoint passing to trigger a combination attack system. Their outside hitters are big and strong, and they can side-out despite an off-target pass.

Directive: Against this team we will serve conservatively. We don't want to risk errors by serving tough. We're not going to gain that much of an advantage with tough serving, because they side-out well, even when their passing breaks down. Instead, we'll keep our serves "in" and cut down on the number of times we give up a point-scoring opportunity because of a serving error.

Deciding on a Starting Lineup

One of the first items to address in designing a game plan is the starting lineup. This may seem on the surface to be a simple matter, and this would be true if athletic talent and positional skill were the only criteria for deciding who should be on the floor. But a team must function as a unit during the match. Each piece must work in harmony with the others. To obtain this desired cohesiveness, a coach must look beyond mere physical ability. A coach must also know the psychology of each player.

Each player must be evaluated according to the team chemistry roles—stud, winner, and stabilizer—discussed in chapter 6. If an athlete does not contribute in one of these ways to the overall team chemistry, no matter how physically talented, that athlete does not belong in the starting lineup. The history of sports is liberally sprinkled with examples of championship teams that clearly did not boast the greatest individual talent. But these teams had in common a special blend of team chemistry that allowed them to function as a unit, weather any storm, and stand tall when it was time to put forth their best effort. Do not be blinded by the sparkle of athletic ability when it is not accompanied by the psychological attributes that potentiate team chemistry.

Some players are better suited to be substitutes. Again, an understanding of the psychology of each player is important in making this evaluation. Is the player emotionally fragile, needing constant encouragement to sustain focus and competitive drive? This type of player probably lacks the consistency to be a starter, but might do well as a spot player. And there are players who are very steady performers but who tend to tighten up under the pressure of critical rallies late in the game or the match. This type of player can function well as a starter but should be replaced when the critical points are played. Some players are front runners, some are fighters, and others are calm, low-error players, who have a settling effect on the team. And then there are the make-something-happen players, who tend to be great substitutes for times when your team is slipping into a deep sleep. You must evaluate your personnel to determine whether they will function better as starters or as substitutes.

And finally, every coach should locate a reliable substitute who always lifts the team's level of play when he or she enters the match. These players are not called starters, but their contribution to the team's success is every bit as important. Where would the Los Angeles Lakers have been without Michael Cooper, the Phoenix Suns without Eddie Johnson, or the Detroit Pistons without Dennis Rodman? Each of these players became famous for the sixth-man role they played with their respective teams. They were essential to the success of their teams. I had two such players on my Illinois team from 1985 to 1988, Sandy Scholtens and Chris Schwarz. Both are short in stature (Sandy is 5 feet 7 inches tall and Chris is 5 feet 5 inches tall), and they were used primarily in substitute roles throughout their respective careers. But my team always played better when either was inserted into the game. They both performed with a great deal of focus and inspiration. Together, they were responsible for more victories than most of their taller and more talented teammates.

Guidelines for Designing the Plan

I recommend three basic guidelines when preparing to design a game plan. They are listed in the box.

Game Plan Design Guidelines

- Present the information in a rotation-by-rotation format. The game is played in six different segments (rotations), and it is helpful to organize the presentation of information accordingly.
- Don't overload the athletes. Limit the number of major game plan directives. Three to five is a manageable number. This means that you have to be highly selective in drawing from the scouting report. Focus only on those items you feel will have the greatest impact on your chances to win the match.

(Cont.)

Game Plan Design Guidelines (Continued)

> • The manner in which the plan is presented is very important. The graphics must be clean, accurate, and neatly drawn. The plan should be written out (ie., typed) and there should be enough copies for all players and coaches. It must be a document that reflects care in its preparation and the importance of its contents.

A Sample Game Plan

The following is a sample game plan taken from my files.

Game Plan

1. _Illinois Starting Line-up_   _Opponent Starting Line-up_

#2 = Setter   #15 = Right Side
#8 = Left Side   #9 = Left Side
#10 = MB   #12 = MB

2. _Serving_
   a. Serve #8 (their top outside hitter) when she is in a front-row attacking position. This limits her attack options.
   b. Serve deep in Rotations 5 and 6. Their passers line up in a very shallow formation, and they have trouble passing the deep serve.
   c. Serve to #9's left (down the line) in Rotation 1; she has a difficult time passing balls to her left.

3. _Blocking_
   a. Match our best blocker (#1) against their best middle hitter (#12).
   b. Take away #8's line shot and channel her crosscourt into our best digger.
   c. Block #10's body line. She always hits in the direction from which she approaches.

4. _Defense_
   a. We will play a perimeter defense. This team likes to hit the ball hard and rarely tips.

5. *Offense*
   a. Our setter can dump the ball to Area 1 on the second contact when #8 serves. She stands behind the baseline when she serves and doesn't get to her Area 1 defensive position in time to defend against the setter dump.
   b. Their #10 is a small but quick (laterally) middle blocker. We will attack her with 1 sets and combinations in the middle of the net.
   c. Their #12 is tall and not as quick laterally. We will attack her with 3 sets and spreads.

6. *Miscellaneous*
   a. Our opponent seems to gain momentum when they begin to string together some stuff blocks. Don't allow this to happen. If we get stuffed once or twice, make sure we momentarily go to an off-speed or tip attack that will take their block out of the picture.
   b. Our opponent is a streaky team. They tend to score and give up points in bunches. Endure their scoring streaks and patiently await our chances to score. We will win if we remain emotionally stable throughout the match.
   c. They like to serve tough. It is the heart of their game plan. They are willing to risk a high number of errors to get their aces. Do not let their aces demoralize us. They will make as many errors as aces. Every time they commit an error think of it as their handing us two consecutive chances to score with our serve.

This plan certainly does not include all of the information my staff and I had gathered on this particular opponent. But it gives you an idea of the kinds of items that can be translated into game plan directives. I should add that included in every game plan is a six-court rotation sheet that diagrams the opponent's serve-receive patterns and offensive tendencies in each rotation. Most players like the security of having this information and use it to familiarize themselves with their opponent.

COACHING THE MATCH

My preparation to coach a match has changed dramatically over the years. When I began my career at Pitt, I was forced by circumstances to burn up most of my prematch energy playing the role of event manager. I had little time to prepare to coach the match.

I began by sweeping the gym floor and setting up the nets. I then braced myself for a 2- to 3-hour ordeal of having to defend my volleyball "turf" against an army of pick-up basketball players, who regularly threatened to dismantle me, my net set-up, or both if I didn't let them onto the floor. Shaken and beleaguered, I also had to set up the team benches, position the scoring table, pull out the spectator bleachers, find the scoresheets and lineup sheets, place a last-second call to the officials to make sure they would show up, unpack the game programs (which I had previously typed and run off on the copy machine), locate and inflate the game balls, make sure the PA system was on and operating, cue up the cassette tape of the national anthem (making sure, of course, that the portable tape recorder's batteries were still good), and, finally, carry in the boxes of T-shirts from the trunk of my car so they could be sold at the match as a fund-raiser for our program. When 6:15 rolled around and it was time for me to conduct the prematch meeting with my players, I was usually exhausted and highly stressed. I rarely found myself in a relaxed enough frame of mind to communicate anything helpful to my team. I think they understood this and, to their credit, found ways to compensate for the woeful prematch environment that I had been forced into creating for them. I used to refer to this experience as the home court disadvantage.

Things are much different for me now. Because I have a highly efficient support staff, I can devote most of my attention to preparing for and coaching the match. I like to break down match-related activities into prematch, match, and postmatch phases.

Prematch Responsibilities

From an organizational point of view, it is essential that you operate according to a clearly defined, staff division of labor. Everything must run smoothly at match time. The tasks, as I have broken them down at Illinois, are shown in sections II/E and II/F of the outline of tasks in the Appendix to chapter 6 (see p. 158). Each assistant coach is assigned a share of these tasks.

Personal Preparation

I have learned over the years that I must approach each match with a relaxed frame of mind. So I spend a good deal of time on match day avoiding stressful situations. Early in the day I practice relaxation techniques. I visualize situations that might come up during the match, and I see myself responding with the right decision and with emotional control. I also use affirmations to train myself to overcome the weaknesses and vulnerabilities I know I possess as a coach. I tend to avoid the office, because I am all too familiar with the hornet's nest of tasks and problems that demand my immediate attention when I am there. In fact, whenever possible I like to play golf early in the morning. Now *there* is a perfect start for nurturing a relaxed outlook on the day of a match.

As the day wears on, I start looking at videotape of our opponent and reviewing the scouting report and game plan. I rarely see anything new during this review, but I like the sense of familiarity and confidence it provides. And finally, I take stock of the particular mood I happen to be in. I have learned that my mood may or may not be the right one for motivating my team. Sometimes I feel light and goofy. But we're playing a crucial match, and the players need a more serious and focused coach setting the prematch tone. Or I might be in an irritable frame of mind, and the situation calls for a more lighthearted approach to things. Or more importantly, I might be feeling anxious over our chances to win, and the players may be feeling confident. The last thing in the world I want to do is threaten that confidence by carrying *my* uncertainties into the team meeting. I have learned to adjust my behavior when my mood is not congruous with what my players need to get ready to play a particular opponent.

Match Day Schedule

I believe it is important for a team to follow a regular routine during the hours preceding a match. The routine we follow at Illinois for a 7:30 p.m. match start is shown in Table 7.3.

Table 7.3 Match Day Schedule

3:15	Pregame meal
5:00	Training room open for treatment
6:00	Staff meeting
6:15	Team meeting
6:30	Team visualization and affirmation session
6:50	Warm-up

Match Responsibilities

At the beginning of this chapter, I claimed that how a coach handles a match can play a decisive role in the outcome of that match. I would like to identify six areas—I'll call them game-coaching skills—that I think are important to a coach's ability to influence who wins.

Implementing the Game Plan

Game plans, no matter how simple or how complex, are essential. They provide a map by which the coach charts the course for the team during the match. To effectively implement the plan, a coach must

- have a thorough knowledge of the plan;
- possess adequate recognition skills, which manifest in the ability to evaluate the team's performance in relation to the plan and to recognize when adjustments are needed;
- manage substitution patterns that correspond to the plan; and
- keep staff and players focused on the plan despite distractions.

Maintaining a Consistent Identity

As coaches, we must take a careful look at how we are perceived by our teams during a match. Our demeanors have a significant impact on our teams' outlooks. I continue to be a student of the coaching profession, and I look with an inquiring eye at the performances of my colleagues. The following is not an uncommon scenario.

The match begins with an enthusiastic warm-up. The coach is smiling, shaking hands, exhorting players to get ready for the big push, and chatting in a friendly fashion with officials. The pregame huddle is handled in a calm fashion as the coach carefully reviews essential features of the game plan. Early successes in Game 1 find the coach firing up off the bench with a raised fist, yelling "Yeaahhh, nice job!" The team responds to this emotionally charged feedback by playing with increased confidence.

But then the match begins to turn. The opponent has found a rhythm and begins to challenge. The coach's gestures of support turn to scowls and frowns. Positive feedback gives way to increased criticism as the coach enters the early stages of "washing the hands" of the entire matter. The forward-leaning, alert posture on the bench is replaced by a crumpled, slouched, disinterested figure of a head coach who has psychologically abandoned his or her players. The facial expressions, body language, and tone of voice have the effect of saying to the team, I've done everything I can, and all you can do is go out there and make me look like a fool; I'm disgusted with you and you're on your own from now on. What a change from the person who coached during the warm-up and Game 1.

Realizing the impact our behavior can have on our players, it is important that coaches carefully cultivate an identity that will enhance rather than detract from their team's chances to win. I don't think the behaviors themselves are as important as the fact that a coach—once a style is pieced together—must be consistent within that style. You can be calm and task-oriented (like Tom Landry or John Wooden), or you can be more emotive (like Bob Knight or Bo Schembechler). You can actively become the focal point of a coach-centered atmosphere, or you can sit back and become the behind-the-scenes manager of a player-centered environment. In the end you have to be yourself. But in finding that self, it is important that you work very hard at nurturing consistency. Your players must know what to expect from you at match time. Otherwise you become a distraction and make the task of winning more difficult.

Focus

I can tell a great deal about coaches by watching how they react in a match moment-by-moment. At one end of the spectrum is the coach who watches—a mere spectator, groaning over each error and applauding each good play. This is an unfocused coach who doesn't see beyond the surface of the game and can express nothing more than knee-jerk reactions to each point or side-out. At the other end is the focused, insightful coach who sees through to the fundamental components of the game and can zoom in quickly on its critical elements.

As we sit on the bench, we perceive the match as an undifferentiated mass of data. We see players attempting to execute offense, officials making calls, hitters being blocked when least expected, balls hitting the floor when they should have been dug, hurried moments of communication, tactical changes by opponents, the end results of plays, the emotional ebb and flow . . . . This undifferentiated mass can overwhelm us, but we can learn to select certain items for focus. This is one of the most important realizations any coach can make. We can choose what we want to focus on during a match.

The box on the following page shows some preliminary recommendations for improving your focus as a coach.

Monitoring the Psychology of the Match

 One of the most valuable insights Pang WuQiang left with me was his feeling that every match "has a different life." A coach must be prepared to react to any conceivable turn of events. On some nights, your players

---

How to Improve Your Focus

• Don't watch the flight of the ball during play. Select specific player movement patterns—your team's base-to-read movement efficiency, for example—and watch them with an evaluative eye.
• Learn to watch the match *by rotation*. This means knowing at all times which rotation each team is in.
• Keep an eye on your opponent's blocking and defensive system. Be immediately aware of any changes.
• Watch the opponent's coach and setter during dead-ball periods. What are they trying to communicate to their team?
• Look for tendencies in the opponent's style of play; are they trying certain things tactically that will require an adjustment by your team?

---

are feeling confident and your opponent is demoralized. On other nights, the opposite is true. Sometimes both teams are playing confidently, while at other times both are struggling. Officials' calls, injuries, mood swings of players or coaches, the atmosphere in the arena, even the weather—all these things interact to make each match a genuinely unique experience. It is the job of the head coach to assess each situation and try to steer the team toward a victory.

I know about this because I have made some colossal mistakes. The most notable took place in 1981 at a tournament at the University of the Pacific in Stockton, California. My New Mexico team was on the verge of a Top Twenty ranking, and we needed a big win. Our semifinal opponent was 10th-ranked Arizona State, and we were gunning for the upset. We won the first game in a surprise 15-6, followed by a shocking 15-0 victory in Game 2. I didn't know how to handle shutting out such a quality opponent and finding myself up 2-0 in the match. My players were feisty and ready to dust ASU in Game 3. It was one of those nights when everything was going right for us.

And then, I opened my mouth. "Watch out," I told them before the third game. "Something weird usually happens after 15-0 games." The life of this particular match was being played out in favor of my team, and all I had to do was sit tight and my players would stampede their way to a win. But no, I had to bring their momentum to a halt by planting the seed of doubt. They looked at me in the huddle with stares of "What?" The whistle blew before I had time to explain, but the damage had been done. My brief, off-the-wall warning was just enough to distract my team. Arizona State won the next game 15-2 and eventually won the match in 5 games. I had blown it, and I knew it.

A coach must strive to keep a finger on the psychological pulse of the match. We can't always make a difference, but we have to behave as though we can. We must always try to be one of the reasons our team wins. And we must never be the reason our team loses.

Keeping the Role of Officials in Perspective

This may seem like an unlikely topic to be addressed as one of the six critical skills for being a good game coach. But the frequency of improper and unnecessary reactions to a referee's decision is so widespread among volleyball coaches that it deserves attention.

I have not always been successful in handling officials' calls with appropriate grace and diplomacy. In fact, I used to be one of the real hotheads on the bench. I would become infuriated whenever I thought my team was getting the short end of the stick. Coaching this team is my life, I rationalized. How can this incompetent fool waltz in here and butcher things so badly? I felt entirely justified, verbally tearing into the evil demon who had wronged me and my team.

As the years passed, I slowly began to realize that I was embroiled in a closet drama. My emotional outbursts were a measure of my own immaturity. I was thinking only of my own disappointment and sense of injustice. I rarely stopped to evaluate the impact my behavior was having on my team. Finally, I realized that my self-righteous reaction to "bad" calls had become a major distraction and that I had to tone things down considerably. I still felt the same surge of anger and frustration at the calls, but I began to train myself to respond in a more controlled fashion. Every time I felt the surge begin to rise I would get up, walk to the water cooler, get a drink, and walk back to my seat. By the time I returned to the bench, my emotions had subsided to a point where I could control them.

Eventually, through practice, I was able to change this very distracting behavior. The frustration is still there, however, and I continue to train myself to react with control. My latest gimmick is to use every referee's call against my team as a cue to check our upcoming side-out formation and to signal the best attack sequence to my setter. The result is that my team can direct their attention immediately to winning the side-out, without having to endure the distraction of a self-serving head coach embroiled in a temper tantrum with an official.

In my opinion, arguing with officials rarely yields a positive result. You are not going to get an official to change a call. In fact, you may invite a more adversarial posture from that official. Officials are human beings and do not appreciate being humiliated or second-guessed. It is true that officials make errors, sometimes serious errors that may cost your team a point, a game, or even a match. But I do not believe that referees intentionally take aim at any one team or coach in making their calls. The unpredictable role of officials is simply a necessary part of competitive sports. And the wise, mature coach must find a way to handle their decisions—no matter how unjust they may seem—with grace and diplomacy. This is best for your team over the long haul.

Situational Skills

Every coach should prepare a set of working solutions for the various problematic situations that arise frequently during matches. A coach should never be caught empty-handed when any of the following situations occur.

Time-Outs

When should they be called? How are they managed? Who is allowed to speak? How does information from the coaching staff get from the clipboard to the players? Should they be coach-centered, or should the players be encouraged to provide input?

Critical Moments

A coach must develop a feel for when the critical moments in a match occur. Sometimes they occur early in a game with the score tied at 3-3. Both teams have sided out several times, and the team that breaks first will probably lose the game. In another game, the critical moment could be when your team trails 10-12 after coming back from a 2-9 deficit. If you can tie the game at 12, you'll probably go on to win. The decisions you make at these critical moments will have a significant impact on the outcome of the match. You should rehearse your moves well in advance so that you feel confident and in control when these moments occur.

Handling the Unexpected

It seems that every match is accompanied by an unexpected turn of events. Your setter sprains an ankle; your top hitter can't find the court; you're team is in the tank, and you're losing to a team that you should be drilling; an argument between two of your starters is carrying over into the match, and the team chemistry is suffering—these are examples of the kinds of things you should be prepared to handle. Anticipate them and be ready with solutions. Otherwise you'll be blind-sided and staggering around looking for an answer. By the time you find one, it may be too late, and the match too far gone.

For years during matches I carried a notecard entitled *What If* . . . . On it I had written out possible solutions to all of the unexpected occurrences I could think of. In the heat of a match, a coach can be overwhelmed by input and the pressure to make a decision. It was helpful for me to have anticipated many of these situations and to have, on a simple notecard, reminders of various ways each could be addressed.

Postmatch Responsibilities

The aftermath of an athletic contest is a genuinely unique occasion. The locker room atmosphere can range from the uninhibited joy of a victory celebration to the funeral silence of a painful loss. Each player and each coach brings a distinct emotional flavor to the situation. Some are hyper-expressive, their highs and lows of the extreme variety. Others are more even-tempered, and one has to pry to find out what they are feeling. Those who have performed well go about their business with a quiet satisfaction, while those who have not are smoldering over their mistakes. Generally, the postmatch locker-room setting—win or lose—is a cauldron of emotional energy. The head coach's job is to evaluate each postmatch situation and deliver an impromptu speech that will focus all of that energy and catapult the team forward toward its next task.

Ingredients of the Postmatch Meeting

I can think of five important ingredients for a successful postmatch meeting.

Emotional Direction

This is the head coach's most important task. You must read the situation. Are you facing a group that is emotionally locked-up, angry and frustrated? Or is your team behaving in a relaxed, contented fashion? What you do and say in the locker room after the match sets the tone for how the team moves forward emotionally. You must be a model of how you want your players to handle winning and losing.

Performance Evaluation in Relation to Game Plan

The coach should review the game plan, item by item, and provide thorough feedback on the team's effectiveness in implementing that plan. The postmatch meeting is the perfect setting for this review, because the experience is fresh in everyone's mind.

Time for Player Input

I believe strongly that players should have a chance to speak out regarding all team matters. I routinely set aside time during the postmatch meeting for players, especially the team captain, to address any issue that may have come up during the match. Many critically important items, from clarifying movement patterns in our system of play to resolving disputes between players, have made it to the floor during these meetings.

Directives for Next Team Responsibility

I think it is important that all team personnel receive explicit instructions regarding all upcoming team responsibilities, such as practice sessions, team meetings, travel arrangements, study sessions, and so on. I want everyone to leave the locker room knowing clearly what happens next.

Reminder of Postmatch Behavior

I frequently find it helpful to remind my staff and players that we have a responsibility to behave in a gracious and appreciative fashion to the many fans and supporters who routinely await the team's appearance after the postmatch meeting. Given the variation in fatigue levels, mood swings, and self-esteem that can follow intense competition, it is sometimes difficult to put on a public-relations face. But I remind them that it is a necessary part of being associated with our program.

Purpose of the Postmatch Meeting

The postmatch meeting is a time for reiterating all that your program stands for, for reaffirming goals, and for offering assistance to those who might be faltering in their quest for success. It is never a time for the indiscriminate unleashing of anger and frustration. This can only result in leaving everyone with a feeling of failure and demoralization. On the contrary, whether after a great win or a tough loss, you are responsible for making sure that your players leave the gym feeling good about being on your team and looking forward to continuing with you in pursuit of the team goals.

Wrap-Up

Many factors determine the level at which your team will play, such as the talent of your athletes, the volume and quality of technical training they receive, their overall strength and conditioning, and whether or not you have designed a system of play that highlights your players' abilities. But learning to *apply* all of these factors—fine tuning the dial so that everything comes into proper focus for your players at match time—is the skill that separates the top coaches from the rest. Practice is a necessity, but not a sufficient condition to bring about a victory. You must also be a good match coach.

Index